p: 1974

PROVO A STORY of PEOPLE IN MOTION

MARILYN McMEEN MILLER
JOHN CLIFTON MOFFITT

BRIGHAM YOUNG UNIVERSITY PRESS

Library of Congress Cataloging in Publication Data

Miller, Marilyn McMeen, 1938-
Provo: a story of people in motion.

Includes bibliographical references.
1. Provo, Utah — History. I. Moffitt, John Clifton, 1896- joint author. II. Title.
F834.P8M54 917.92'24 74-3483
ISBN 0-8425-0882-1

Library of Congress Catalog Card Number: 74-3483
International Standard Book Number: 0-8425-0882-1
Brigham Young University Press, Provo, Utah 84602

Printed in the United States of America
74 2.5M 17382

CONTENTS

ACKNOWLEDGMENTS

Credit for the inception of this history belongs to John C. Moffitt, who gathered the original materials together and convinced the city and the Brigham Young University Press to publish this project. Much of the careful information collected by Mr. Moffitt has been compiled into updated lists in the appendixes. His foresight, attention to detail, and ability to correlate and organize made the project possible. From his work, further efforts by many other Provoans have resulted in the finished product.

For the suggestion that the work be primarily a pictorial account, and for the careful editing of the final manuscript, we are grateful to Gail W. Bell, and for reading the materials through the various manuscript stages, we wish to offer appreciation to James B. Allen.

Many people helped to obtain the outstanding pictures. O. Blaine Larson gave freely of his father Thomas C. Larson's special collection of early photographs, and Nelson Wadsworth, who was in possession of many of the glass negatives at the time of publication, generously copied many of them at a minimum of expense. We appreciate David Dinsdale for his leads in obtaining photographs, as well as for offering a few historical details that made the account more interesting, Rell G. Francis for the prints from his collection, and John W. Bun Taylor and his wife Alta for their patience in making it possible for us to photograph their prize album containing snapshots taken by Mr. Taylor's father, Walter G. Taylor. Dale H. Price from San Gabriel, California, also donated a few old prints to John C. Moffitt for our use.

We appreciate N. La Verl Christensen for generous use of the Provo Daily Herald's collection of photographs, and Joseph M. Boel for prints of the old fort paintings from Mr. Christensen's history of the meetinghouse and tabernacle. For photographs of modern Provo we wish to give credit to the Provo Chamber of Commerce, Provo City, and the Provo Daily Herald and their photographers. A few prints were also collected from the archives in the City and County Building, and the Provo City Public Library.

Also, we wish to thank Michael Kawasaki for his careful work in design and layout, and the workers at the Brigham Young University Photo Studio, Press, and Printing Service for their careful efforts in every phase of the production of the work.

Without the financial and moral support of the Provo City government, the project would not have been possible, and we wish to thank the city officials who participated in offering their help.

Marilyn McMeen Miller

ONE

A CHOICE VALLEY

Because Brigham Young was ill on his journey west, he kept his wagon a little apart from the others. In the bleak Wyoming countryside near Fort Bridger some distance away from the main camp, he had a conversation which helped decide the destiny of the Mormon people. Lying or sitting on his bed, he requested his guest, the grizzly mountain man Jim Bridger, to join him for a warm meal. Inside the privacy of the wagon Jim Bridger and Brigham Young talked for hours, far into the night. Jim Bridger told Brigham Young everything he knew about the valley: the best routes the wagons should take to enter it, the kinds of grasslands, streams, and timbers the settlers would find.

It was from Jim Bridger that Brigham Young learned the location of the Ute Indians. They were camped in the Utah Valley south and east of the great Salt Lake in what Bridger declared were the choicest lands of the area. Bridger warned Young: "The Utah tribe of Indians inhabit the region around Utah Lake and are a bad people. If they catch a man alone they are sure to rob and abuse him if they don't kill him . . . They are mostly armed with guns."[1] Bridger advised that Brigham Young shift to the north on his way into the valley, and settle near the great Salt Lake, a "no man's land" between two tribes — the Shoshones on the north and Ute Indians to the south.

Brigham Young listened to what Jim Bridger had to say. His original plan was to colonize the entire area, to send groups of people up and down the valley, both north and south. There would have to be some encounter with Indians, but perhaps for now it would be wise to stay away from them.

From this evening's conversation the Mormon leader decided to make his first settlement northward in the location of today's Salt Lake City. When nearing the valley, he dispatched a letter to Orson Pratt, who was several days in advance of the Young party, and told him to bear north because the Ute Indians were likely to be "a little tenacious about their choice lands."[2]

Had it not been for Jim Bridger's warning, the first settlement may have been more to the south than what it was, perhaps as far south as the present location of Provo.

Other Whites into the Utah Territory

Although the Mormon people were the first whites to settle in Utah Valley, they were not the first whites to visit there. Probably the earliest and best known group to enter the area was the Escalante-Dominguez Expedition. On 29 July 1776 Father Sylvestre Feliz de Escalante and Father Francisco Acunasio Dominguez, two Christian friars, left Santa Fe, New Mexico, with ten men in search of a route to Monterey, California. It is not known why they traveled so far northward, turning east at a point near the Utah-Colorado line, unless guides deceived them, or they hoped to encounter the Indians of this area. Nevertheless, on September 23 they found themselves in Utah Valley.[3]

Escalante was so impressed with this area that he wrote extensive descriptions of it in his diary. His men were awed by the mountains that surrounded the valley, the excellent quality of the soil, the abundance of grass, grain, and flax. They praised the beauty of the streams that emptied into the lake, the cool nights, and the pleasant days. They were perhaps most impressed by the Timpanogos Indians (*Timp* "rock," and *Nogos* "canyon people"). As the friars taught these natives about Christian doctrines, they found them to be a responsive and friendly people. Escalante writes of wanting to return immediately to New Mexico, gather a group together, and return to this valley to set up an array of Christian villages along the mountains of the Wasatch Range.

The friars continued southward through most of Utah toward California, but as winter was approaching and the weather was beginning to grow cold, they turned back to New Mexico rather than continue their search for Monterey. Although they were never able to fulfill their plans to return to the area and convert the Indians, their work in exploring was not in vain. Their maps and guides and extensive descriptions of the countryside served as good material for traders and trappers who came through later on what was known as the Old Spanish Trail.

Slave Trade

For years after the Escalante-Dominguez expedition, Spanish and Mexican traders would come up into the Utah Valley and trade with the Indians. One of the major items of trade was Indian slaves. Mexicans would bring food, guns, and other items into the valley and take away with them Indian children and women. They would in turn trade these slaves to miners on their way to the California coast for a good price. The Mexican government tried to put a stop to this inhumane practice, but slave trade continued for seventy-five years, even to the times when the Mormons were settled there.

A story is told of Mauricio Arze and Lagos Garcia, who were taken to court in Mexico to be tried for slave trade with the Indians. They pleaded innocent, however, saying that so eager had been the natives to

With the exception of fences, roads, and barns, the valley of the Utes probably looked much like this. *Courtesy of O. Blaine Larson.*

trade slaves with the Spaniards that they threatened to kill their horses if they did not buy.[4] The high prices that were paid for potential slaves encouraged the Indians to perpetuate the traffic in this human product.

Etienne Proveau, Mountain Man

The slave trade was equalled only by fur trade. Several fur companies came into and through the Utah Valley bringing with them colorful mountain men. One of the best known was Etienne Proveau, the man after whom the Provo River and later the city of Provo were named. Little is known of his early years except that he was born in Chambly, Quebec, Canada, in 1785. He spent most of his adult life in different expeditions trapping in the Rocky Mountains. Although most of them were private expeditions, he was with the American Fur Company on the Missouri River, and with other organized groups from time to time.

Proveau is often credited with the discovery of South Pass and Salt Lake, although there is no absolute proof of this. However, he was well known as one of the major trappers of Utah Valley. As he and his partner LeClerc were trapping along this river during the fall of 1824, the fame of one of his experiences gave the river its name. An evil Indian called "Bad Gocha" invited the Proveau-LeClerc party of about fifteen trappers to sit with him around the fire and smoke the calumet of peace. As Indians and whites sat together in the darkness, the Bad Gocha stopped his ceremony and declared he could

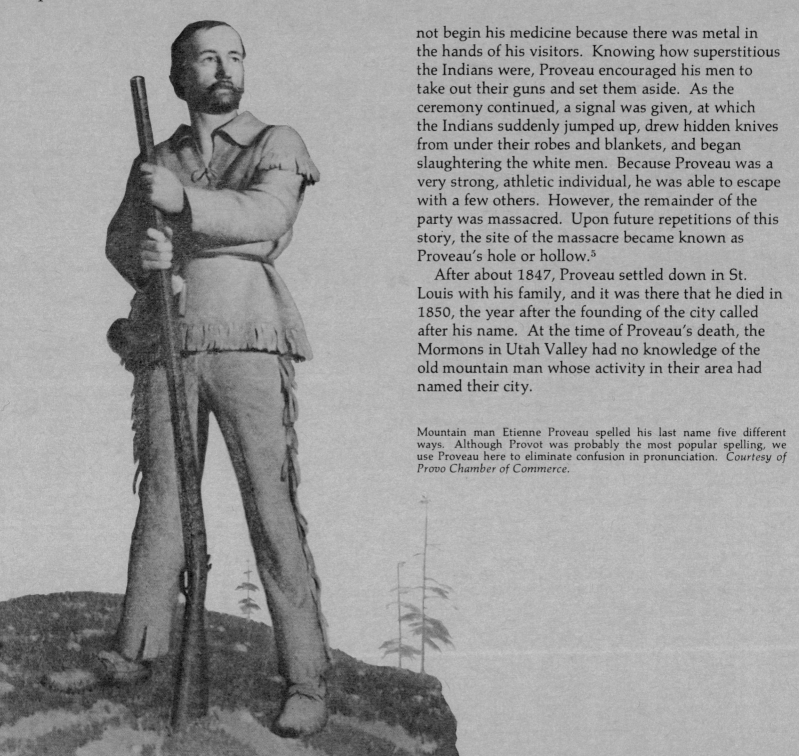

not begin his medicine because there was metal in the hands of his visitors. Knowing how superstitious the Indians were, Proveau encouraged his men to take out their guns and set them aside. As the ceremony continued, a signal was given, at which the Indians suddenly jumped up, drew hidden knives from under their robes and blankets, and began slaughtering the white men. Because Proveau was a very strong, athletic individual, he was able to escape with a few others. However, the remainder of the party was massacred. Upon future repetitions of this story, the site of the massacre became known as Proveau's hole or hollow.[5]

After about 1847, Proveau settled down in St. Louis with his family, and it was there that he died in 1850, the year after the founding of the city called after his name. At the time of Proveau's death, the Mormons in Utah Valley had no knowledge of the old mountain man whose activity in their area had named their city.

Mountain man Etienne Proveau spelled his last name five different ways. Although Provot was probably the most popular spelling, we use Proveau here to eliminate confusion in pronunciation. *Courtesy of Provo Chamber of Commerce.*

TWO

MOVING IN ON THE INDIANS

Exploring Utah Valley

Because the Mormons had been driven from Missouri and Illinois by hostile mobs, they were anxiously looking for a new home where they would find peace. They hoped this faraway isolated valley would offer them plenty of room for growth free from outside problems.

After their arrival, they did not waste any time before they sent explorers to the surrounding areas, including Utah Valley, to investigate the countryside and particularly to discover the nature of the Indians. On 28 July 1847 Orson Pratt stood in the Oquirrh Mountains and looked southward on Utah Lake. Other explorers took a boat on wheels toward the lake, but found it difficult without more teams and men to make it through the Jordan narrows. In December, after Parley P. Pratt's wheat was planted, he and several associates went to Utah Lake with a boat and fishnets; although their success with fishing was poor, they learned more about the valley.

It was not until 6 January 1849 that the Church sent out a group on a specific mission to investigate using the valley as a cattle range. Forty or fifty men were to take the large group of cattle for grazing; they were also to seek a suitable place to establish a fish hatchery.

The First Battle with the Indians

Although it was decided to send cattle down into Utah Valley, the decision ultimately marked the beginning of trouble with the Ute Indians, for they

The original Fort Utah was located at the right of this spot on Provo River. *Courtesy of Provo City.*

began to steal the cattle. By the end of February the Indians had caused so much trouble that a company of thirty-one men, under the leadership of Colonel John Scott, was sent down to put a stop to the rustling.

As the militia came into the Utah Valley, they found the Ute Indians very excited, angry, and frightened. Their leader, Little Chief, was friendly, however, and told them that he would help them find the outlaw Indians who were stealing their livestock. Little Chief's son guided the militia through the foothills. After approximately six miles, the militia found the outlaw Indians camped on what is now Battle Creek in the area of Pleasant Grove. Dividing into four parties, they surrounded the small camp and waited until daybreak.

When the Indians awoke and saw that they were surrounded, they began frantically shouting, "Go away or we will fire!" The militia ordered the Indians to come out and surrender, but they would not. When the arrows began to fly, the whites began to shoot. Squaws and children waded into the creek and crouched in freezing water while arrows and bullets whizzed over their heads. Determined to die rather than to surrender, the Indians tried to hold their defense, firing from behind bushes and the banks of the creek, but they were soon routed out. All of the braves except for one young boy were killed.

When the militia returned to camp and told Little Chief what had happened, the chief wept. Although he had sealed their fate by sending his own scouts, his heart was filled with pity for these, his own people, who had come to such a bad end. Moaning and screaming, the chief smote his breast, blaming himself for what had happened.

Settlers Sent to Utah Valley

Although the campaign against the guilty Indians had been successful, the Church authorities were disturbed by the nature of the massacre. They were afraid this event would mushroom into more Indian troubles.

Immediately after the incident at Battle Creek, Brigham Young determined to send families to settle the Utah Valley area. He hoped that if the whites began to live peaceably among the Indian nations, they might teach the braves to cultivate the land and to become a civilized people. At a council meeting on 10 March 1849 Brigham Young called thirty men to settle the valley.[2] By the end of March thirty-three colonists were ready with arms, equipment, seeds, clothing, pots and pans, ox and horse teams to make

This painting portrays Samuel Jepperson's interpretation of the appearance of Fort Utah at its original location south of Provo River and about 300 feet east of the present Geneva Road. Note the spacing of the houses, and the raised cannon in the center. *Courtesy of Joseph M. Boel and N. LaVerl Christensen.*

their way southward. They were instructed to settle quietly in the valley, to be cautious and patient with the Indians, and, if possible, to live with them in peace.

When the settlers arrived just three miles north of the place they were to build their first fort, they were met by an excited young brave called Angatewats.[3] Riding toward the approaching caravan rapidly on his horse, he blocked their trail, and told them not to come farther. Dimick B. Huntington, a member of the Mormon Colony and serving as interpreter, ultimately convinced the brave that they meant no harm. He asked the young man to give them a chance to talk with the other Indians. To the larger party Mr. Huntington expressed the desire of the settlers to live in peace. He swore they would not drive the Indians away, or take away their rights.

Moving into the choice lands of the Indians was a risk for the settlers. However, Angatewats and the others allowed them to move down the Provo River and camp for the night. The very next morning they began to build Fort Utah.

Building a Fort; Farming

Measuring 20 × 40 rods, the fort was a rectangle of individual log houses built just a few feet apart, with entrances facing toward the center. In the spaces between the houses tall pickets imbedded into the ground fashioned a sturdy outside wall that protected the settlers. In each house were two cloth-covered windows. There were gates at both the west end and the east end of the fort, and in one corner a corral

Some of the original log cabins of Fort Sowiette are still preserved at Sowiette Park. *Courtesy of Provo City.*

where the cattle were kept during the night. In the middle of the fort, the men erected a bastion where they placed some 300-pound cannons.[4]

As soon as the fort was built, the people laid out 225 acres of land, began irrigating it, turning it over with their crude plows, and planting food. Although it was springtime the settlers had great difficulty. Heavy spring snowfall and late frost worked against them. And while they were waiting for their wheat to sprout, they were cut off from the Salt Lake Valley by extremely high waters in the Provo. It was almost a year before their crops got a good start. There were some hungry times for those early colonizers.

Old Bishop

During those first years, however, their greatest concern was their relationship with the Indians. On 4 July 1849, six men organized a militia to appease the uneasiness in the white settlement, but in August an incident occurred that caused the Indians to be very angry.

Three white settlers on their way out to hunt cattle found the Indian "Old Bishop" wearing a fancy shirt. One of the white men, Richard Ivie, claimed the shirt was stolen from a clothesline, and he demanded to have it at once. Old Bishop loudly protested that he had bought the shirt, which so angered Ivie that he tried to tear it off. Immediately Old Bishop drew his bow and began to shoot. One of the other settlers standing by whipped out his gun and shot Old Bishop in the head, killing him. The white settlers took Old Bishop's body, filled his abdomen with rocks, and threw him in the river. The Indians found his body only 24 hours later.[5]

Outraged, the Indians came to the fort and demanded the life of the man who murdered Old Bishop. When they were refused satisfaction, they began to shoot the cattle with their bows and arrows, killing some of them. The white and Indian tension was high.

As the 49ers on their way to California came through the valley, more serious trouble developed. The prospective miners traded guns and ammunition with the Indians in return for slaves. Now, armed with good weapons of offense, the Indians continued shooting and killing cattle with zest, calling the white people names, threatening them when they left their homes to go out into the fields.

Life Goes On

However, through all of this trouble the settlers seemed to maintain some resemblance of normal life. They worked, farmed, ate, and socialized. They even held parties.

Occasionally without shoes, they gathered on the dirt floors of private homes to enjoy rousing dances. For lights they placed their knives in between the chinks of the logs in the cabin walls and placed

Another painting by Samuel Jepperson depicts Fort Utah under construction in 1850 at its second location near the present Sowiette Park. *Courtesy of Joseph M. Boel and N. LaVerl Christensen.*

candles on the knives. Someone always had a fiddle handy, and there was gay laughter, music, and good fellowship.

From the beginning the settlers met in close-knit church and civic meetings, sharing prayers daily and making plans for the development of their new community. It was in these daily and weekly meetings that issues were discussed relating to the establishment of a city charter, a schoolhouse, and a city council. Mary Turner set up a little school in one corner of the fort and began to teach the children. Capable men began to build a sawmill and a tannery. At the time of his visit on 14 September 1849 Brigham Young found a busy, progressive community.

The major change that took place on Brigham's first visit to Provo was the relocation of the fort. Because Fort Utah had been built so close to the river, the fields were constantly plagued by flooding. Brigham Young rode with a few others to a spot about two miles southeast of Fort Utah, including the area where Sowiette Park is now located, and declared that this was the place the people should begin to build their city. The men laid out a square mile to be the heart of the city. They surveyed and plotted blocks of four acres each; the center block was arranged for building a chapel and a schoolhouse.

When he left, Brigham Young admonished the people not to be familiar with the natives, but to build good walls around the new location, to keep inside the fort, and to take responsibility for themselves. On 27 November, when Parley Pratt passed through

the settlement, he found 57 log houses built on 17½ acres of ground in the new location.[6]

Battle at Fort Utah

The change in location and Brigham Young's warnings, however, did very little good to curb the Indian problem. The Indians would come up to the fort windows, look into the people's homes, and make hideous faces. They shouted at them, calling them old women and cowards who were afraid to fight. They also killed the cattle and continued to shoot if the settlers were out alone. Finally on 31 January 1850, the weary pioneers sent two men, Miles Weaver and Peter Conover, to Salt Lake City to plead their case before Brigham Young. They wanted permission to confront the Indians.[7]

With Brigham Young at the time was Captain Howard Stansbury, a United States topographical engineer there for the winter to do some surveying. He convinced Brigham Young that fighting the Indians was probably the only answer. He felt his surveying would not go as he planned unless the Indians were taken care of. On 2 February Brigham Young announced that he would allow the settlers to subdue the Indians in Utah Valley. The following day George Grant and a company of volunteers met and organized in Salt Lake City. After a long march toward Fort Utah they arrived there on 8 February.

On the morning of 9 February 1850 they began their campaign against the Indians. They found them hiding behind a bank in the river and also occupying a log house that had been deserted by James Bean. They had given so much trouble to Mr. Bean that he

Big Elk and his squaw were important participants at the Fort Utah Battle. She is the one whose fall from Squaw Peak gave it its permanent name. *Courtesy of John W. Bun Taylor.*

had finally let them have his property.

As was their custom, the settlers at first tried to settle peaceably. Their interpreter, Dimick B. Huntington, asked the Indians to powwow. Ope-Carry, the Indian spokesman, came out and began to talk with Huntington. But while the two were talking, the Indian Big Elk began to shoot, and the whites returned fire.

Because the Indians were hidden and protected by the log house, they were difficult to overcome. At the end of a long day of shooting they still held their defense. Several of the Salt Lake militia were wounded. On the following day the whites determined to take the log house where the Indians were hiding. They charged across the river ice but, in the process, seven or eight of their horses were killed. Groups of militia tried to enter the house from both the back and the front. Another group built a barricade of logs, placing blankets on the inside of it so that bullets which pierced the logs might bounce against the blankets. Using this barricade on wheels as a mobile tank, they rushed toward the Indians. Frightened, the Indians began to run. However, as they fled, they cut hunks of horse meat from the bodies of the horses that had been killed.

Many white men were wounded. One man with a large nose had left his house in the morning with a warning from his wife: "If you will be shot, it will be your nose." Unfortunately, her warning was accurate; he was shot in the nose.

After they left James Bean's log house, the main body of Indians split into two parties. The smaller party went with Big Elk toward Rock Canyon. When Big Elk was killed on the way, his bereaved squaw, in trying to escape, fell from the mountain and was killed. Today that location is called Squaw Peak.

The larger party of Indians retreated toward Spanish Fork, finally arriving at Utah Lake, where they tried to escape across the ice. As they were pursued, they would lie down as if dead and, when a settler drew near, rise up quickly and try to shoot. In spite of these tactics, all the Indians were killed.

The icy lake is the scene of Dr. Blake's unusual surgery. At a more recent date Provo people used the ice for refrigeration, cutting it out in winter and keeping it stored in caves during the summer. *Courtesy of John W. Bun Taylor.*

One of the men in Captain Stansbury's survey party, a surgeon by the name of Doctor Blake, expressed a desire to take the skulls of these Indians to a medical institution in Washington. He asked two young men to go with him out on the lake with a sleigh. One of these young men wrote a colorful account of what happened. According to his report, as they came to an Indian, Dr. Blake got out his surgeon's instruments and carefully proceeded to cut off the head. The two young men waited impatiently in the bitter cold while Dr. Blake did his deed.

By 14 August 1903, the date of this reunion of Indian war veterans at Utah Lake, these men who had participated in the Indian wars were grandfathers with big families. *Courtesy of Rell G. Francis.*

The photo at right, probably taken in the early 1870s, looks northwest on Center Street. Taylor's furniture store, located by the tree, is shown in more detail on page 19. *Courtesy of Provo Chamber of Commerce.*

Finally, when the boys saw that the doctor wanted not just one head, but several, they decided to take the operation into their own hands. Quickly they took out their knives and began chopping the heads off with great speed. In a matter of minutes, while Dr. Blake stood back and watched them, they finished the job.

The decapitating foray was not the end of Dr. Blake's curious investigations. Next he shot some ducks; he gathered them up, feathers, entrails, and all, and placed them in the box with the heads. He instructed one of the young men to bring the box "in a week or two to Salt Lake City." In the written account the one young man writes, by that time ". . . the weather turned warm and the ducks were green with rot. [T]he Indian heads smelt loud." When the young man reached Dr. Blake's office with the unusual package and told him the ducks were spoiled, he said the doctor took a wing out of the box, smelled it and said, "Hmm, it's just right." Then he invited the boy to dinner. The boy writes, " [I] was not hungry and declined his offer."[8]

Of course, the Indians were not happy about their defeat at the battle near Fort Utah. However, the incident did curb their harassment of the settlers, and they remained somewhat peaceable — except for skirmishes among themselves — until the latter part of that next July. It was in July that Chief Walker returned from California with 1,000 stolen horses. Refreshed by his recent successful raids, Walker's thirst for power was high, and he asked Brigham Young for help in fighting the Snake Indians. Brigham Young refused. Angry, Walker brought his horses to the fields surrounding the Provo fort and threatened to massacre the settlers. Frightened, the people watched their crops being trampled and destroyed by the hundreds of horses. They were not sure what would save them.

Sowiette Saves the Settlers

It was at this time that their friend, the Indian Sowiette, warned them of Walker's plans and came to their rescue. Sowiette told Walker that he would not allow him to fight the whites, and, if necessary, he and his own men would stand to protect them even until death. That night some bullets whistled over the fort, but no one was hurt. Finally Walker, Sowiette, and both bands of Indians went away together. This incident gave Sowiette Park its name and brought attention to the kindness of this Indian.

This building is the original Third Ward meetinghouse and seminary, located on the northwest corner of First North and Fifth West. The existing Third Ward assembly hall was built immediately north of it in 1901. *Courtesy of John W. Bun Taylor.*

The City Grows

Although Indian troubles still continued, the little settlement began its business of becoming a city. On 31 January 1850, the general assembly of Deseret named it for the first time "Provo," and declared the town to be the county seat of the newly created Utah County. On 6 February 1850, the town was granted a city charter which provided for the election of officers. Immediately they elected Ellis Eames the mayor, along with four aldermen and nine councilors. Although George Albert Smith did not live in Provo at the time of the election, he had been appointed by Brigham Young to look after the city, and so he was also chosen to be a member of the city council. When he arrived in Provo with one of his families in August, 1852, the people enthusiastically built a house for him, which he later returned to them for use as a seminary.

Soon the two small forts were not large enough to hold everyone, and the settlers began to build homes on the lots laid out in the city. The log schoolhouse was moved from the old fort and placed in the public square where two wings were added to it. Two hotels were built. To keep up with the improvements in the city, the new city council passed ordinances insisting on fence repairs, clean timber areas, and one free day's labor at periodic times from every male citizen on the roads. George Albert Smith's presence fired the energy of the settlers to build many industries. By the end of December in 1852 there were two grist mills, a pottery, three cabinet shops, a sash factory, a wooden bowl factory, three shoemakers, two tailor's shops, a meat market, two stores, two lime kilns. The company known as the Deseret Manufacturing Company had begun to make plans for raising sugar beets on 1,000 acres of land.[9]

Still, the settlers joined in at parties and weddings. At their dances they served homemade cake sweetened by corn and beet molasses. They ate berries and raisins, custard pies, and nut cakes. To pay for the fiddler they would often purchase tickets during the day with squashes or pumpkins. They also put on plays and organized choirs for their church meetings.

Provo's first official choir began at a church service in 1851, when the presiding officer had some difficulty in starting a hymn. William J. Strong, a recent convert new to the settlement, simply announced a hymn and began to sing. When his English friends around him joined in, the number was so successful that there was a rousing request for a repeat performance. Mr. Strong was named Provo's first official chorister.[10]

Ellis Eames was Provo's first mayor. *Courtesy of Provo Daily Herald.*

Walker War

While the business of becoming a city occupied the people of Provo, the Indians kept a reasonable distance until two unfortunate incidents occurred in the summer of 1853. In the first, a group of Indians begging for some food from Mrs. Young threatened her with a gun. The Indian holding the gun accidentally shot one of his own companions, and the Indians ascribed the deed to the whites.

In the second incident, an Indian squaw approached James Ivie at his house and asked him to give her some flour in exchange for some fish. As they were trading, the squaw's husband, in company with some others, rode up to them. Angry with his woman either for trading with the white man at all, or for not getting a good bargain, he lashed out at her, beating and kicking her. Ivie tried to stop him, which made an accompanying Indian angry enough to draw out his bow and arrow. Ivie grabbed the arrow and hit the Indian on the head with his gun. Ivie's blow was fatal, for later the Indian died in camp. Although the whites had tried to make peace with gifts, Walker's Indians were very angry. On 18 July, they killed a guard at Fort Payson and precipitated what is generally known as the Walker War.

With the beginning of these Indian hostilities,

This 1879 photograph of Center Street shows the completion of the back half of a building only partially completed on page 13. *Courtesy of Provo Daily Herald.*

Brigham Young ordered the people to occupy their forts. On 20 July Peter Conover went to Payson with a militia of 150. Attacks by the Indians were made at Springville, at Nephi, and in Sanpete County. They seemed determined to fight. Brigham Young wrote to Walker, "I send you some tobacco to smoke in the mountains when you get lonesome. You are a fool for fighting your best friends, for we are the best friends, and the only friends, that you have in the world. Everybody else would kill you if they could get a chance."[11] However the fighting mushroomed and continued into the early fall.

In Provo one of the most belligerent Indians was one named Squash who claimed that his brother had been buried by the people without Indian traditions. Angry, Squash demanded payment in blankets and cattle. Not being able to pay him right away, the settlers tried to appease him but he would not be appeased. The Indians were angry when the settlers put Squash in prison, where he died shortly afterward. Some say that a guard killed him. Some believe he killed himself.

While the fighting continued, the people tried to build a wall around the city. It was to be twelve feet high, six feet wide at the bottom, tapering to a two-foot width at the top, with an eighteen-inch rock foundation. As the fighting died down, progress on the wall was slow. It was never completed.

Making Peace with the Indians

The settlers hoped that methods other than building walls would solve the Indian troubles. Once they tried giving a feast for them. They killed and roasted three cattle in a giant picnic held in what is now the park on Fifth West and Center Street. The women mixed up three barrels of biscuit dough, made pounds of butter, and cooked up a great load of squash. The Indians enjoyed the feast, but it was not enough.

Near the time of the feast, two young boys in Cedar Valley had been murdered by two Indians, and Brigham Young had requested the two murderers be brought to justice in the courts. While the people of Provo were doing everything in their power to try to improve Indian-white relationships, their efforts were negated when the Indians became angry because the two murderers of the boys were publicly executed on 15 September.[12]

Although the Indians continued to raid, the death of Walker helped to curb their harassment. Walker died at Meadow Creek near Fillmore on 29 January 1855. With Walker's death his brother, Arrapene, became leader of the tribe. Arrapene claimed a vision in which Walker told him not to fight with the Mormons but to settle peaceably with them.

Following the Walker War two other major battles were the Tintic War, a raid on the west side of Utah Lake against some difficult Indians, and the Black Hawk War, which took place much later in the areas south of Provo. However, after the Walker War, the major difficulties with the Indians — at least for the Provo settlers — had ended.

THREE

THE SETTLERS ARE TRIED

The end of the major Indian troubles was by no means the end of trouble for the people of Utah Valley. The next chapter of Provo history reads somewhat like the story of Job. The townspeople were beset with problems that at times seemed almost insurmountable.

Famine

The grasshoppers had been bad in 1854 but in 1855 they were overwhelming. The sky was literally black with insects.[1] After devouring the first crops, they seemed to simply wait until the people planted again, and then returned to devour the second crops. Women and children took blankets and tablecloths out into the fields and beat the grain to save just a little for themselves.

That year, as though an answer to their prayers for food, a saccharine substance fell on the leaves of the trees. Men, women, and children gathered this substance from the trees and boiled it to make sugar. The events of these years read a great deal like the histories of the people in the Old Testament; the townspeople were certainly tried as though in the same proverbial "wilderness."

Not only was the harvest bad, and as a result the grain scarce and expensive, but the winter of 1855 and 1856 was an extremely difficult one. In that year, after such poor harvests, the handcart immigrants of 1856 came into the valley, cold and hungry with no food for themselves. The settlers in Salt Lake City and Provo had a difficult time sustaining the immigrants. In general there was a great

After so carefully planting their crops in this wilderness valley, the Provo farmers met with the discouragement of grasshoppers and late frosts. *Courtesy of Dale H. Price.*

deal of hunger and suffering. A typical story is that of Samuel Jones's wife, who one day for lunch brought him only a small piece of bacon and some greens; the promised bread was missing. When Samuel asked her about it, she burst into tears, admitting she had been so hungry she had eaten it on the way. The young couple cried together in each other's arms.

During that time, as people met one another they would say: "Have you got your breadstuff?" This was the common greeting of the day. If a person answered "Yes," he was considered well to do.

Reformation

Perhaps the Church leaders felt that a rededication to the Lord would help to improve the trying circumstances. Whatever their thinking was, they initiated a new reformation in the autumn of 1856 in the hopes of inciting the people to live a more disciplined and religious way of life. All over the valley — in Salt Lake City, Provo, and all of the settlements — people were rebaptized in a motion of commitment or recommitment to God and their Church.

The United States Army Arrives

Then, as though the trials of Indian and famine were not enough, out from the East came the strong arm of the United States Government to put even more disciplinary measures upon the already buffeted pioneers. President James Buchanan in the summer of 1857, misinformed by troublemakers who told him that the Mormons were in open rebellion against the

United States Government, ordered a militia to proceed to the Utah Territory to terminate Brigham Young's governorship and put the Mormons in their place. This news worried the settlers. Brigham Young told the captain in advance of the army, "We do not want to fight the United States, but if they drive us to it, we shall do the best we can; and I will tell you, as the Lord lives, we shall come off conquerors."[3]

Several groups of Mormon militia attempted to harass the United States troops before they reached Salt Lake Valley, but even without harassment the army would have been unable to penetrate the mountains before winter snows set in. They had to stop at Camp Scott, a few miles from Fort Bridger, and set up quarters for the winter.

During the next few months, Thomas Kane, in defense of the Mormons, tried to convince Buchanan that they were not a rebellious people. He encouraged the new governor, Alfred Cumming, to come to Salt Lake City and find out for himself the truth about the Mormons. Many were afraid for Cumming to risk the trip, but on 12 April 1858 he reached Salt Lake City to govern the people and settle the situation with the approaching army.

When Cumming arrived, he was undoubtedly surprised to come upon floods of people migrating southward.[4] The Mormons had decided they would not be present when the army advanced on them that spring. They left their homes stacked with straw so that a few who were left behind could set fire to them if they felt it was necessary. Wagons loaded with goods, cattle, and women with their children in their arms were all trudging wearily toward Provo. A young woman said, "We left our comfortable homes with the expectation of never looking upon them again. I need not say we were sad and almost heartsick. . . . After a so happy respite from driving we were once more upon the move!"[5]

This is a close-up of the George Taylor furniture store seen at a distance in the photographs on pages 13 and 16. *Courtesy of Provo Daily Herald.*

Alarmed at the giant exodus, Cumming tried to assure the Mormons there would be no problem, but he was too late. Thirty thousand people brought their high-piled wagons into Utah Valley to camp in the city of Provo.

This event in Provo history was one of its more colorful ones. Crowds of people took refuge in Provo homes; a large tent was set up in the center of the public square where Brigham Young and the others kept offices and a storehouse. When the summer became hot, the water grew bad, and the crowded quarters became uncomfortable.

A Mr. Farr writes ". . . we had to dig holes to get water, and the people began to complain of sickness. The feed had also been all eaten off by the cattle, our cows dried up, flies were very bad tormenting our cattle, and it was with great difficulty that we controlled our stock from running off."[6]

Utah County's first courthouse and jail, completed in 1867, was located on the block between First and Second East and First and Second North, where the woolen mills were built, and P. E. Ashton's stands today. *Courtesy of O. Blaine Larson.*

It was not until 30 June 1858 that Brigham Young finished negotiations with Cumming and convinced the people that they could return to Salt Lake City. The army, which was now approaching the valley, did not commit any hostile actions but crossed the Jordan River and camped about 37 miles southward at Camp Floyd.

With the presence of the United States troops the Mormon people, although they had now returned to their various homes, were still uneasy. United States judges from the East, still certain that the polygamous Mormons represented a dangerous threat to the American way of life and the constitution by so closely combining church and state, set up courts in various areas to try the people. A Judge Sinclair convened court in Salt Lake City in October of 1858 and tried to sentence the people on grounds of treason and polygamy. He did not put many in prison, however. In Provo Judge Cradlebaugh, known later as "One-Eyed Jeffries," caused many problems for the Provo settlers. When he convened his court, he astonished the people by bringing in 100 soldiers from Camp Floyd. He explained to the citizens that the presence of this militia would save them from having to construct a jail. However, it is thought that he secretly believed the presence of the army and the successful court sessions would encourage the Mormon people to overthrow their despotic government and set themselves free.

Instead, the Provo citizens were enraged. Insulted by the presence of this "walking calaboose," they demanded the removal of the troops.[7] However, in reply, Judge Cradlebaugh simply ordered up 900 more men from Camp Floyd. Finally on 14 March Governor Cumming came to investigate this situation. He told General Johnston, who was now in charge of Camp Floyd's army, to withdraw his troops, but General Johnston said he had instructions to cooperate with the judicial government as well as with the executive. Cumming protested with the attorney general at Washington. While the troops were in Provo, Cradlebaugh tried the people in court for various crimes, but he was unsuccessful in convicting them. Finally by the time word from Washington arrived that the troops should be withdrawn, Johnston had already decided to return them to Camp Floyd.

The withdrawal of the troops was a gala affair. Sixteen platoons of infantry that had been camping on the outskirts entered the city to join the others. Coming in by the north gate, they marched southward down Main Street while the martial band played "Doo Dah." At about three blocks south of the seminary they made an about-face and commenced the return march while the band played "The Girl I Left Behind Me." Eight more platoons of infantry joined them at the courthouse on the corner of what is now 1st North and 5th West, and the grand military expedition began its way to Camp Floyd.

This view looking west on Center Street shows the same building on the corner of First West which presently houses the Stone Drugstore. *Courtesy of O. Blaine Larson.*

The Troops: A Help and Hindrance

Perhaps this incident of trouble with the troops in Provo was one of the reasons the federal government in Washington agreed to reduce the army at Camp Floyd. Whatever the reasons, when the army left the valley the people of Utah felt relieved. The troops had been unruly and noisy and in general a nuisance to the church-going Mormons.

Not everything about the army's presence was negative, however. The one thing the army did do was to stimulate the economy. At the disposal of government property, about $4 million worth of government goods were sold for $100,000.[8] At this time merchants bought goods to resell at profit-making prices.

Perhaps the only people partially sorry to see the troops go were the businessmen who had lined their wallets with money by trading with the soldiers. One of them, Samuel S. Jones, had begun his profitable mercantile business in Camp Floyd, first by making adobes for the fort and then forming a partnership with William Daly to provide vegetables for the camp. The first item the partners tried to sell was a load of green peas. They sold so slowly that Daly became discouraged and gave up. Samuel Jones persisted, however, until he sold every pea and made a profit of five dollars. This success brought Mr. Daly back into the business, and they sold vegetables to the soldiers during the remainder of the summer.

Provo was not without its saloons. This one was located at 57 North 100 West. Identified in the picture are, from left to right: David Nelson, Israel Hodson, Willard Booth, Hyrum Harrison, two unidentified men, David Vincent, and Samuel Richards. *Courtesy of O. Blaine Larson.*

After the army left, Samuel S. Jones, who then bought a business and went into a partnership with a Jewish merchant Benjamin Buchman, was later to play a significant part in the development of cooperative merchandising in Utah.

Although the economic stimulation which the troops brought to the area was in some ways favorable, in other ways it simply proved to be another trial.

It was during this time that the liquor business became a problem in the city. Although the city council had passed and amended an ordinance in 1855 and 1858 to assure the regulation of liquor sales, they passed an even more stringent ordinance in 1861, and in February of 1862 ordered the marshal to remove Chatwin's distillery, which had become a real nuisance. Shortly after this the council, now reduced by legislation in 1862 to one mayor, two aldermen and three councilors, gave one of the city aldermen the exclusive right to make and sell liquor so that sales would be better controlled. For years afterward there was trouble between private parties who applied for licenses to sell liquor and those in favor of city control and prohibition.

As much as the city fathers tried to curb the liquor problem, the federal troops in Provo had stimulated early patterns for drunkenness, wild parties, and salty behavior on the part of quite a few people. Perhaps the hardships of their early years were too much for some of them to bear in a dignified way, or they were simply too busy fending off Indians, famine, and federal troops to pay very close attention to such problems as social culture and education.

Schools and Culture

At any rate, early interest in education got a slow start. Little school construction had been done in

The members of Provo Third Ward had their pictures taken on 25 April 1901, at the laying of the cornerstone for their new building, the present Third Ward assembly hall on First North and Fifth West. *Courtesy of O. Blaine Larson.*

The old and the new stand together. *Courtesy of Provo Daily Herald.*

1854 when George A. Smith said, "The citizens of Provo need their energies stirred on the subject of schools," nor had they done much even as late as the year 1860 when a new settler, William Miller, was so alarmed by the lack of organized schools that he offered a reward to the five districts in Provo if they would each build a schoolhouse.[9]

A clipping from the *Deseret News* of 5 September 1860 reveals the circumstances clearly:

> Education and educational institutes are somewhat below par in Provo. I think I may safely say, there is not a ward school house in the city. Sometime ago a great excitement was got up in the Fourth Ward in regard to building a good school house. Meetings were held, speeches were made, a committee appointed and the thing was to be done forthwith; but, alas! for the stability of human enthusiasm, the summer heats have wilted it, and a few leads of rock laying on the ground, is all that can be seen of the noble structure.
>
> . . . Our boys and girls are running wild for want of proper training and culture, and I think a school room a most proper place to bestow the labor necessary to develop the youthful mind, and I may confidently assert that if the time which has been loafed away and the money which has been spent at and around Whiskey Point during the past year and a half had been devoted to public improvement a good schoolhouse might have been built in all the wards of the city.[10]

It was not long after William Miller's arrival that each ward responded and built a schoolhouse. One of Provo's most outstanding educators, Warren N. Dusenberry, was the teacher in the first ward school after his arrival from California in 1862. He built his own furniture for the children and with his own money purchased $50 worth of books. Mr. Dusenberry and his brother Wilson gave lectures for the teachers, advocating less harsh methods of discipline and encouraging them to create appealing lessons. These two brothers raised the educational atmosphere in the city to a higher level.

Increased activity in drama and music followed the concentration on education. In 1864 the city council purchased instruments to stimulate musicianship in the band which had been organized since 1856 by an Italian, Professor Ballo, from Salt Lake City. The Amateur Dramatic Company was organized at a meeting held in the second story theater of Cluff's Hall on 27 April 1861, at which time the members decided to purchase some scenery from Camp Floyd, which became available at the timely exodus of the troops and also to set forth some objectives in presenting plays. Some early dramas performed were *Still Waters Run Deep* and *Deaf as a Post.*

There was no doubt after the withdrawal of the federal troops, the relaxation of Indian troubles, and the establishment of schools that culture, along with economic stability, began to take hold in Provo. Perhaps a single date that marked the end of a long period of troubles with hostile outsiders might be 8 June 1865. On this date the whites celebrated, with bands and parades, the settlement of the Indians on their own lands apportioned to them by the U.S. Government. Other celebrations mark the increased spirit of having conquered the environment. On Utah's twenty-first Pioneer Day, at a big barbecue in 1868 attended by Brigham Young, Provo sang an original song written by Samuel S. Jones to a tune composed by L. John Nuttall. The words are a revealing expression of their pride in their new homes.

May every heart in Utah's vales
Be jubilant and gay
Nor let the shades of bygone cares
Becloud our holiday.
This day it is the twenty-fourth;
'Tis Utah's natal day;
So cheer for liberty and Utah.

Chorus
Hurrah, hurrah! 'Tis Utah's natal day;
Hurrah, Utah is twenty-one today.
Compare the present with the past
Success has led the way —
And cheer for liberty and Utah.

We'll not forget today,
To applaud the pioneer,
Who stared grim famine in the face,
Met trials without fear,
And served the crickets, wolves, and snakes
That once resided here
With notices to quit the vales of Utah.

Nor will we fail to memorize
Battalion boys so true,
Who left their wives and country
To fight in Mexico.
For this blest country of our choice,
The old Red, White and Blue,
And prove to all our loyalty to Utah.

In the early 1860s polygamist Bishop Aaron Johnson built a twenty-seven room home for his many families. *Courtesy of O. Blaine Larson.*

The gold fields all around have tried
To lure us from our home,
Forsake our honest industry,
For fantasies to roam;
But we think we've found the color
In our grain fields' fertile loam
And struck a lead to happiness in Utah.

Now let us cheer for Brigham Young,
Our faithful Mormon guide,
And cheer for all the faithful Saints
That in these vales reside
And now a long, long, hearty cheer
For Utah's natal tide
While Heaven is smiling on Utah.[11]

Brigham Young so well liked the stanza about the grain fields in preference to the gold fields that he asked for it to be repeated.

In spite of their early struggles, it seems the people of Provo were finding much of their "happiness in Utah."

FOUR

HERE COMES THE WORLD

Although the people of Utah were relieved at the exodus of Johnston's army, they had only begun to see the fruits of what the world-at-large would bring into their community. With the completion of the railroad at Promontory Point near Ogden in 1869, it became clear the Mormons were not going to be able to stay in an isolated paradise built only for those who believed the same as they did. The world was moving in on them. Already the influence of Johnston's soldiers affected the young men, who began to participate in drunken and rowdy behavior.

The Church Tightens Controls

Concerned about the social, spiritual, and economic welfare of the Mormon people at the advent of the railroad, Brigham Young took early precautionary measures to fortify the "saints" against encroaching outside influences.

Laboring under fly-by-night reports from the East that the railroad would be "used as an agency to break into pieces the Mormon Church,"[1] Brigham Young took several major steps to strengthen the Mormon communities.

One of the first things he did for Provo was to call the prominent pioneer Abraham O. Smoot to the office of president of the stake and "bishop of Provo City." The Smoot family journal reports the event of this appointment with an often repeated standard joke:

> A. O. Smoot was doing well in Salt Lake City when Brigham Young called him in and said, "I'm

This excellent view of the old Provo meetinghouse in relationship with the Provo tabernacle is from a snapshot taken by Walter G. Taylor from the lot where J. C. Penney's stands today. The big tower in the center of the tabernacle was removed in 1917 because its weight was causing the roof to sag. The bell in the tower became the old "Y" bell that still hangs on campus. *Courtesy of John W. Bun Taylor.*

going to call you on a mission. There are three places, all on a par. One is as good as the other. They are Hell, Provo or Texas. You can take your choice." A. O. replied, "I would sooner go to Hell than to Provo." Apparently he didn't give a second thought to Texas.[2]

After his arrival in Provo, Smoot was immediately elected to serve as mayor along with his church appointments, cementing the relationship of church and city government for the next twelve years. Smoot's arrival was just one of the efforts made in Provo at this time to tighten the Church and increase religious zeal in the area. Just the year before, Provo had completed the construction of its new meeting house on tabernacle square. It had been a slow project — begun in 1852 at the site of the old Pioneer Park on 5th West and Center Street. Brigham Young suggested the meetinghouse be moved to its location on the southeast corner of University and Center, where on 24 August 1867 he dedicated it in a conference session. This was the meetinghouse which was later torn down in 1918 after the present Provo Tabernacle was built in 1883. However, a monument to its existence stands near the present Woolworth building. On 9 February, following its dedication, Smoot was sustained as stake president, and in a Provo conference session in October Brigham Young's exhortations included a plea for Church members to maintain economic self-sufficiency. Fearful that the railroad would bring in money-hungry entrepreneurs, Brigham Young

Looking east on Center Street gives us a good view of Provo's East Co-op building. To the far right behind the wall is the site of the Provo library. The little house behind the white placard in the far background is presently the home of Maternity Wardrobe. *Courtesy of O. Blaine Larson.*

suggested the Mormons trade only among themselves. He soon afterward suggested cooperative merchandising and thus launched the great economic movement in Utah that in some areas culminated in the United Order.

After Brigham Young had exhorted Mormons to trade only among themselves, the Salt Lake City merchants were so enjoying their increased business activities that they were slow to cooperate with each other in general merchandising. It was at this time that Provo played an important part in carrying out Brigham Young's suggestion.

Provo Businessmen Cooperate

One day after a late autumn 1868 Sunday School meeting, Samuel S. Jones, the pea merchant of Camp Floyd days, discussed the possibility of cooperative merchandising with his friend David John. There had already been some cooperative merchandising in Lehi and American Fork. Mr. Jones, an orthodox Mormon who was now in business with someone outside of the Church, saw that he must act quickly if he was to maintain his status quo. Immediately he and Mr. John went to their newly appointed stake president, A. O. Smoot, to discuss the possibility of setting up a cooperative mercantile. President Smoot approved of the idea, and at a meeting on 4 December he met with Mr. Jones, Mr. John, and three other interested citizens, drawing up a preliminary organization to which the group subscribed $5,000. Subscriptions reached $17,000 by the end of December, and on 5 January 1869 the organization

This photo of the Provo Woolen Mills, completed in 1873, was taken near the corner of First North and Second West looking northeast. P. E. Ashton's now occupies much of this block. *Courtesy of Provo Daily Herald.*

was named "Provo Co-operative Institution."

Much interested in what these enterprising Provoans were doing, Brigham Young brought three of his apostles and several other men down from Salt Lake City on 8 February to offer $5,000 for his own stock and further the project. It was in this meeting that a Mr. Lawrence offered his store for $3,000 in stock, and Utah's first cooperative store was established. On his return to Salt Lake City apostle Cannon wrote in the *Deseret News*, "Provo has set an example which Salt Lake City need not be ashamed to imitate."[3] This action by Provo merchants alarmed the merchants of Salt Lake City, who were afraid of being undersold by their southern neighbors. As a result of Provo's quick action, the Zion's Cooperative Mercantile Institution was soon established, which today still carries its name, ZCMI.

It was not long before many of the citizens of Provo were called upon to sacrifice for the success of the cooperative. Even the Relief Society sisters operated the Co-op Store for a time. Samuel S. Jones became agent of the West Branch of the store, and later the East Branch. Both stores maintained successful operation until the panic of 1893.

Although the next step in cooperation, the United Order, never took hold in Provo (though accepted by vote in 1874), the successful cooperative merchandising stimulated the organization of the Timpanogos Manufacturing Company on 1 June 1869. With a capital of $1,000,000, or 10,000 shares at $100 each, this cooperative became the base organization of the Provo Woolen Mills. Brigham

A view of the Provo meetinghouse and tabernacle from University Avenue, the Parker School located at First East and Second North, and a shot of the valley taken from the mountain; in the foreground is the state hospital. *Courtesy of O. Blaine Larson and Provo Chamber of Commerce.*

Young invested $70 in this company. A building was erected in 1870 and machinery purchased in the East and hauled from the railroad to the mill site. Although the people of the area were reluctant to purchase "homemade material," and complained because its quality seemed less than that of imported fabrics, the mills gradually grew in size and capability until by the end of 1874 they were turning out 2,000 yards of material daily and soon supplying carpet for public buildings such as the St. George Temple and Salt Lake City's Representatives Hall.

Increased Industry

Other industries began to flourish during the 70s and 80s. A silk industry was established by Daniel Graves, who initiated the Utah County Silk

Contrast this photograph with those of Center Street on pages 13 and 16. The trees have grown, and so has the Taylor Brother's furniture store. *Courtesy of O. Blaine Larson.*

Association. The townspeople purchased silkworms from France and planted mulberry trees to produce a small amount of silk. At an early date pottery was produced and sold in Provo, as well as adobe bricks for house-building. For years the adobe yard was located in the Sowiette Park area. In 1866 a Mr. Colton built Provo's first kiln, and by 1874 Allen's brickyard was employing ten people and using two mills to mix and grind the material. Many brickyards followed, as well as lumber companies. One of the first major lumber companies was begun by Abraham O. Smoot in partnership with William Paxman and later David John. From the lumber of this company many of Provo's buildings during this period were built: the Provo Theatre, the First National Bank Building, the south wing of the mental hospital, the Parker School, the Stake Tabernacle, and many others. During this period Provo also built the County Courthouse and began to build gravel sidewalks.

Other events which stimulated community progress during this time were the organization of canal companies and the construction of canals to increase irrigation in the area, and in 1876 the organization of the Pleasant Valley Coal Company. In 1877 Milan Packard built a narrow gauge railroad to Springville to serve as transportation for coal. In October of 1873 the Utah Southern Railroad had brought track within seven miles of Provo, and on 25 November, at 10:45 a.m., the first train pulled into town amidst a celebration, with bands playing and people shouting. With the entry of the railroad

THE
CONKLIN
SAMPLINGW

In the above left, the photographer is standing in the intersection of Center Street and First East looking southwest at the county courthouse erected in 1873. This corner is now empty. *Courtesy of O. Blaine Larson.*

A view of Center Street shows both tabernacle and meetinghouse. On the north side of Courthouse Square the tower of the fire station (page 54) is barely visible. *Courtesy of John W. Bun Taylor.*

to Provo there was no question about the presence of the world now.

The newspaper began as a daily, the *Provo Daily Times*, in 1872 under the leadership of John C. Graham and R. G. Slater, and later changed to three times and then two times a week. It was now filled with news of national interest: the world was shrinking around them. Outsiders began to come in. The area was expanding.

Riot

Rowdy behavior was still a problem. An incident in 1870 aroused the citizens to an even greater concern over the liquor problem and the encroachment of the world in general. On 22 September a group of

The Eureka Saloon was one of several on Center Street. *Courtesy of Joseph M. Boel and N. LaVerl Christensen.*

The S. W. Sharp livery and feed stable was located just west of the southwest corner on First West and Center Street. *Courtesy of Provo Daily Herald.*

soldiers from nearby Camp Rollins became unruly when they were denied the use of a hall for a dance. In a state of drunkenness the soldiers came to the homes of Provo officials and stood in the street, shouting and threatening to break into the dance hall. They claimed they would burn it, or tear it down. Finally when they went to the hall they smashed in the doors and windows, and called for the owner to come out. Using bad language, they shouted and called him names. Others who went to reason with the soldiers were held up with pistols and guns. Finally the soldiers released their prisoners, and began to leave, but on their way out of town, shouting and yelling, they broke the windows in some of the homes.

Education

Although the advent of the world brought increased rowdiness into Provo, an increase in cultural and educational activity managed to keep most Provoans civil, educated, and abreast of their times.

In 1869, when Warren Dusenberry returned from a mission, he reconvened his previous school in the Kinsey Building on Center Street. From all parts of the county pupils of third-grade education and over were invited to attend classes. So many responded that it was necessary to move the school to a larger building.

During the winter of 1869, Robert Campbell, Territorial Superintendent of Schools, and George A. Smith and others visited Dusenberry's school. It was

This was the first school built where the present Timpanogos School stands on Fifth West and Fourth and Fifth North. *Courtesy of O. Blaine Larson.*

These normal school graduates of 1892 were some of Utah's future teachers. *Courtesy of Provo Chamber of Commerce.*

at this time they made the school a branch called the Timpanogos Branch of the Deseret University. The enrollment soon reached 300. Other teachers were employed, and the school became so popular and so well established that finally Brigham Young recognized it as a separate institution. In 1875 the authorities of the Church made Timpanogos Branch into the Brigham Young Academy. With a principal, two teachers and 97 students, the BY Academy opened its doors in 1876.[4]

At first Warren Dusenberry continued for a time as principal of the Academy, but he soon suggested the very capable Karl G. Maeser be appointed to serve in his stead. Mr. Maeser, sent down from Salt Lake City by Brigham Young to teach nothing unless it was with the Spirit of God, had been teaching in the "normal school," giving instruction to help educate the school teachers of the area. He was such a capable instructor that in 1876 when Warren Dusenberry wanted to convince the County Court to appropriate tuition money for some students, he made arrangements for the court to visit Karl G. Maeser's classroom. One day in September the County Court dismissed for a time and met at the classroom to hear Mr. Maeser give his lessons. They were so impressed that they responded to Mr. Dusenberry's request by paying tuition for 26 students.[5]

In 1884 the Brigham Young Academy was destroyed by fire. Immediately Samuel Jones granted the use of his business building and later the students met in the ZCMI warehouse, which they divided

Although culture and progress were changing the face of Provo, occasional reminders of the pioneer days still remained. In the background is the north side of Center Street between University Avenue and First East. *Courtesy of Dale H. Price and photographer George E. Anderson.*

into 11 rooms. After the fire, the leaders of the Church and community decided to build the Brigham Young Academy building on 5th North and University, now still in use by Brigham Young University. Other denominations also built academies during this time. The Provo Methodist Seminary opened on Monday, 30 August 1886. The Congregationalists opened the Proctor Academy in 1887. They built an imposing two-story structure on the corner of 1st West and 1st South.

Culture

The increased interest in education sparked an accompanying interest in culture. In 1877 just after the Timpanogos Branch of the University of Deseret was named Brigham Young Academy, popular Salt Lake actor John C. Graham moved to Provo and appeared that December in two hit plays in the Brigham Young Academy building, *All that Glitters Is Not Gold* and *Brother Bill and Me*. His presence in the city stimulated dramatic productions, and in two years two separate dramatic companies were organized. One of the companies, the Provo Amateur Dramatic Union, was composed of members of the Provo Fourth Ward. John C. Graham and other members of the general city population organized the Home Dramatic Company. Both organizations gave plays in Cluff's Hall and competed to get Provo's biggest audiences and most enthusiastic responses. Many in Provo chatted about the plays of each company and followed the competition with keen interest.

Music and drama became important during this period of Provo's history. *Courtesy of O. Blaine Larson.*

For a list of the names of the Brigham Young Academy faculty of 1891-92, see the appendix. *Courtesy of Provo Daily Herald.*

Ten Nights in a Bar Room was ironically the biggest success of the Church company. John C. Graham's group received applause for *Uncle Tom's Cabin* and *The Two Orphans.*

Finally in September of 1880 the two companies merged into the Home Dramatic Company under the management of John C. Graham, and in 1883 the Provo Theatre Company organized and planned to build the Provo Theatre, which was dedicated with pomp and excitement on 24 and 25 July 1885 by a performance of *The Streets of New York.*

Changes in Life Style

The entry of the railroad and, closely following, the influences of the world had had major effects in the stimulation of industry, business, and culture. Although the Mormons had tried to maintain their singular way of life by building many churches and fostering cooperatives, their pioneer ways were rapidly disappearing. Perhaps the final blow which the entering world dealt to them was the interruption of their sacred belief in polygamy.

One of the main events that changed the lives of many of the people was the passage in 1882 of the Edmunds Law, which defined polygamy as a felony. Later the Edmunds-Tucker Act was a more severe action against this Mormon practice. It demanded that Church property be confiscated and that commissioners in government position be required to take a monogamic oath. Raids were made by federal officers in homes where there was known to be polygamy. Many of the prominent men built closets

Utah County Clothing House stood at the corner of Second West and Center Street. *Courtesy of O. Blaine Larson.*

This liquor store stood about where Hoover's is today. *Courtesy of O. Blaine Larson.*

or trap doors that were not seen so they could escape the officers. Abraham O. Smoot maintained hiding places — one in the stake tabernacle and one in a closet in his home on 192 South 1st East in a box under a trap door covered by a rug.[7] During this time many men went to prison in Salt Lake City to pay for what was now described as a crime by the United States Government. The prison was never full of such impressive prisoners. The women and children had to turn to the work in the fields and in the businesses. Finally, on 24 September 1890, Wilford Woodruff, the President of the Church, composed the Manifesto, which disavowed polygamy for the Church members. After the Manifesto, it still took a while for polygamy to die out as a practice, but the lives of the people were permanently changed. Now the community resembled more of an American town than a group of zealous religious people; it seemed now to be a community of people from all denominations who worked in many industries and combined their efforts to foster an increased cultural standing in their personal lives.

FIVE

BOOMING AND LOW TIMES

Boom!

The BOOM began in 1888. On March 20 the *Enquirer*, the Provo newspaper of that time, ran headlines that read, "Boom, Boom, Boom."[1] Entrepreneurs and real estate investors from the East and West had come to Provo and were paying exorbitant prices for real estate. Property on Center Street was bringing $100 a foot; a young couple from the East bought the Excelsior Hotel for $10,000 cash. As a result of glowing advertisements, eastern money began buying houses, lots, and farms. Subdivisions with well-built homes sprang up all over the Provo area. The Provo Chamber of Commerce, organized to stimulate growth in the community, published a 50-page pamphlet describing the "Garden City" of Utah.

Important new people came to Provo. There was talk in the Chamber of Commerce of trying to settle the capital city in Provo instead of Salt Lake City. There was a sudden spurt of energy in all areas of industry and business. Free schools were launched in 1890. The Provo Manufacturing Company, which had become the Provo Woolen Mills, pledged 180 shares into a new electrical system, and under the management of A. O. and Reed Smoot provided power for the city. Waterworks were planned and completed in 1892 by the Rhodes Brothers of Denver. Mr. A. A. Noon built the first cannery. Mr. Thomas F. Pierpont and his son took over the Provo Foundry and Machine Company. Mountain Bell Telephone purchased a twenty-year franchise. The North American Asphalt Company began paving the

During the gay 90s, the Provo Opera House was the scene of many cultural events. Built at the same time as the Provo tabernacle, 1883-88, it was situated at about 40 North First West. It later became the Provo Armory and was torn down in the 1950s. *Courtesy of Provo Daily Herald.*

sidewalks at $10 a ton of asphalt. During this exciting time men became enthusiastic, ready to act, to reach out, organize, and do something.

The number of men's organizations that sprang into being attest to the feeling of action and brotherhood. The Odd Fellows organized on 11 December 1889 with eleven members. Other organizations were the Knights of Pythias, Woodmen of the World, and the Benevolent and Protective Order of Elks.[2]

Gay 90s in Provo

People began to participate in the kind of social activity that launched the entire country into the gay 90s. It was a time of parties, laughter, good fellowship, and material prosperity. During the real estate boom, 11 saloons opened up in the Provo

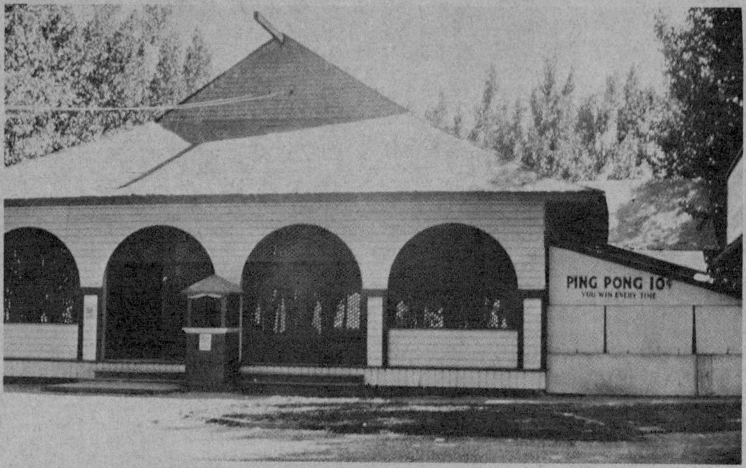

People have always used Utah Lake as a resort, but especially during the gay 90s. By 1921, Geneva Lake Resort was a good-sized complex of recreational facilities. *Courtesy of John W. Bun Taylor.*

Below at the left is a photograph of the small railroad that took Provo people to Utah Lake. Above, the train turns north on University Avenue. *Courtesy of O. Blaine Larson and Rell G. Francis.*

area. People from all over the countryside and out of town came into the city on hayracks and in carriages. For local excitement Provo built a small railroad or streetcar railway out to the lake. On holidays, Saturdays, Sundays, and even weekdays families gathered together and rode the streetcar out to the lake resort, where they swam, boated, picnicked, and basked in the sun. The lake resort included bath-houses, luncheon booths, refreshment stands, and a dancing pavilion, as well as a boat harbor. Floods destroyed it during the time of the panic, and it was never fully revived.

Later, the Geneva Lake Resort was built where the present-day steel company now stands. Clubs held big barbecues, and an early citizen reports, "liquor flowed freely."[3]

Boating

In connection with the Provo Lake Resort, the important and wealthy businessmen of Provo — the "Socialites" — organized the Provo Boat Club. They sent for two regular papershell crew boats 32 feet long and 3 feet wide to be manned by 4 men with 8 oars. When boats arrived in Provo from New York City, there was a gala celebration and ball. The boats were draped and taken to the opera house, where they were to be unveiled with a flourish of pomp and music. The ball on 1 May was one of the most memorable occasions of Provo. Members arrived costumed in the club colors — black and gold. The women of the club presented a beautiful satin flag to the men. William H. King, the president of the club, received the flag ceremoniously, giving a

For good times, these Provo people took the train to the Castilla Springs resort in Springville, where this photograph was taken on 16 June 1905. *Courtesy of Rell G. Francis.*

Many boats were built in Provo for use on Utah Lake. To add interest to this shot, this photographer also included the train. *Courtesy of Provo Daily Herald.* On the facing page is Provo's boat crew.

speech in which he expressed his hopes that the ladies would be present when they won the races. Competing against Salt Lake City, the teams won in both 1890 and 1891. They held some of the races on Utah Lake and other races on Salt Lake, strapping their huge boats to the side of a special train and moving northward with gala cheers — and a Chinese cook. All the Provo participants were outfitted in special uniforms of navy blue trousers and white sailor blouses.[4]

In 1891 Provoans made plans for a pleasant journey across country on transportation that would take them to the shores of Utah Lake, across the lake on a relaxing boat trip, and to the other side by railroad again to the Tintic area. The route was also to be used for freight. Enthusiastically the Provoans built the *Florence* and on 7 May, after a christening speech by Abraham O. Smoot and accompanying music by the Enterprise Band playing "Gee Whiz," the *Florence* was launched at 9:45 with 50 passengers aboard to make its maiden voyage. It was supposed to have met on the other side with a delegation from Eureka, but nobody was there. A little seasick, the *Florence* passengers deposited their freight and made the return voyage. The plans for using this route for major transportation never materialized, and the boat was taken somewhere else in the panic of '93.[5]

Music

There was also a general spirit of increased cultural activities as music became important. In the first year of the boom, the Provo citizens built a band-

PROVO BOAT CLUB
FIRST LIGHTWEIGHT CREW

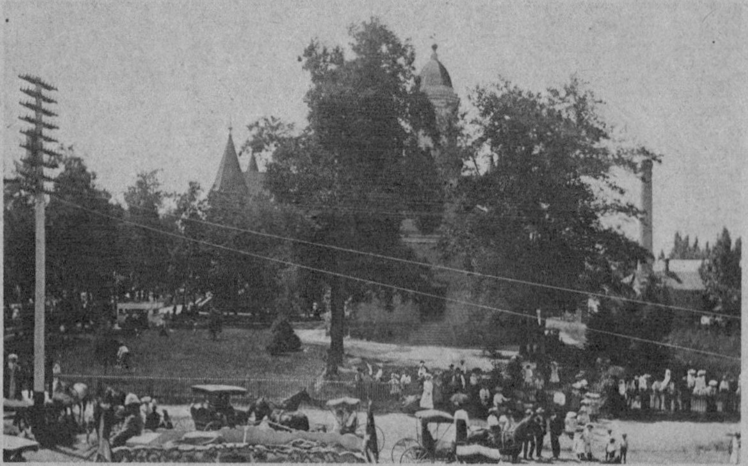

Included in some of the early activities of Provo people were parades, as shown by this commercial float, a sleigh ride in Pleasant Grove, and a circus in Center Street. *Courtesy of O. Blaine Larson.*

Provo's Silver Band included, in the front row: Henry Saunders, Oscar Flygare, William Lewis, Wallace Cottam (?), Lars L. Nelson, and Heber Bridewell Rollins (?), and in the back: Thomas Allen, Owen Johnson, Brigham Johnson, Herman Knudsen, George Peay, John Allen, John W. McAdam, and William Peay. *Courtesy of Provo Daily Herald.*

A list of the singers in this Provo tabernacle choir of 1902 appears in the last part of the appendix.

stand on courthouse square and the Silver Band directed by James H. Wallace gave concerts every Saturday evening during the summertime. In September of 1888 a grand band rally was held. All the bands from the county came to the Provo Opera House for the contest. First prize went to the Payson band, second to the Spanish Fork band. In the evening around five p.m., a grand parade of 135 instrumentalists marched down the street. Then everyone enjoyed a luncheon at the opera house and a gala ball in the evening.[6]

Politics

As well as an increased enthusiasm in social and cultural life, Provo became politically active. For many years, the political division simply consisted of Mormons against non-Mormons, or the People's Party versus the Liberal Party. It was common knowledge that liberals attempted to undermine the political powers of the Mormon officers because they were offended by the combination of church and state that seemed to exist. The climactic moment between these two parties was the election of mayor in 1890, at which time the Liberal Party tried with fervor to elect their candidate, George Sutherland, over John E. Booth of the People's Party. Warren N. Dusenberry was also in the contest, but played a minor part.

For the campaign, the Liberal Party transported a drum corps from Salt Lake City and a drill group, the Flambeau Club. On Saturday evening, 8 February 1890, the drum corps and drill club marched down

Taylor and Poulton grocery store was located between First and Second West on Center Street next door to the W. Freshwater store. *Courtesy of O. Blaine Larson.*

Samuel S. Jones was the innovative merchant who spurred the cooperative effort in Provo. This is the interior of his store in 1892. *Courtesy of O. Blaine Larson.*

the streets followed by jangling, shouting party members. The People's Party responded to the event with seven bands and a huge torchlight procession.

Although Sutherland was not elected as mayor, he became a prominent political figure, and later sat as chief justice of the United States Supreme Court. After this election, the two parties began to align themselves with the Democrats and Republicans.

Panic

The "boom" didn't last very long. During the winter months of 1890 and 1891 only a few of the 16 new real estate dealers renewed their licenses. Suddenly, the people of Provo could see that the investors from the East had not really brought that much money with them in purchasing real estate. There had been too much buying on credit.

It was at this time that the banks closed and businesses began to fail. The depression in this area was simply aggravated by the national panic of 1893. The Provo City Lumber Company failed in 1892 and also the West Co-op Store. In 1893 many more businesses failed including Samuel Jones and the Sun Foundry. Mr. Jones's goods, invoiced at a value of $15,000, netted only $5,500 at a forced auction sale. A number of the eleven saloons went out of business, unable to afford licenses.[8]

When floods destroyed the lake resort, the City Street Railway or small streetcars that had taken so many people after work and Sundays out for recreation closed down. As they failed to operate,

Most of these early photographs of Provo businesses were taken by Thomas C. Larson. *Courtesy of O. Blaine Larson.*

These shots show the exterior and interior of R. A. Barney's store located near First West on Center Street. *Courtesy of O. Blaine Larson and Nelson Wadsworth.*

their franchise was taken from them.

In August of 1893 the city government felt the necessity to discontinue the street lights. Mayor Holbrook, however, offered to light the city for one year by himself; the people gladly accepted.[9]

With the panic of 1893, as industrial armies began marching from the West to the East, many of them came on train through Provo. In one incident a Mr. Carter and an army of marchers stole a train from Union Pacific at Lehi Junction, transferred it to the Denver and Rio Grande tracks, and headed for the East. At Provo, as they slowed down in response to a warning that there were torpedoes on the track, the engine was run onto a switch and derailed. Suddenly Provo found themselves host to about two or three hundred jobless, homeless men. By request of the sheriff of Provo, John A. Brown, Salt Lake City sent down a company of militia to help curb any problems that might occur, and the city of Provo immediately gathered together beef, potatoes, onions, and other foods to feed their visitors. Some of the men deserted the army, some of them continued the march eastward, while Carter and a few of the leaders were put for a short time into the Provo jail.[10]

Rallying

In the face of the panic and its difficulties, Provoans did not give up easily. They simply tightened their belts and dedicated themselves to a more disciplined effort. Excessive partying came to a halt.

Just before the panic, the boom had allowed the building of a new home for Brigham Young

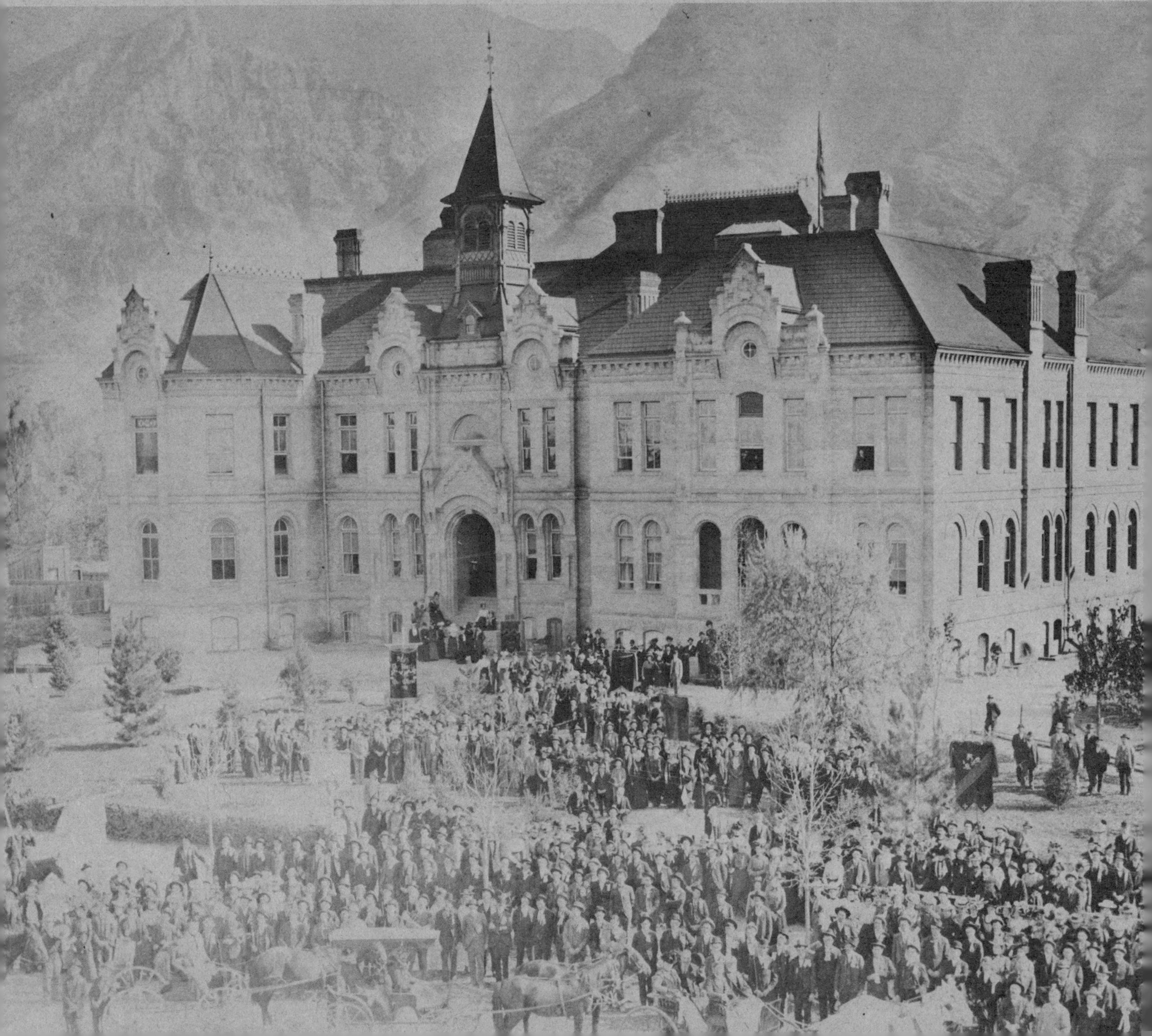

This grocery store and the General Scott barbershop next to it were located at 90 West Center Street. *Courtesy of O. Blaine Larson and Nelson Wadsworth.*

Academy. On 4 January 1892, 500 students marched into the $75,000 education facility, a monument to an increased spirit of dedication and conservatism.

These years following the panic were the years people also buckled down to serious interest in industry. One young man, able to raise himself up out of the depression, was George Startup. An eighteen-year-old boy who in 1895 was the youngest typesetter at the *Daily Enquirer*, George Startup had already established his reputation as a hard worker and concerned individual. Every day his pay envelope went to his mother to help support the family. While the other boys in the plant went to drink or went out to the lake to have their fun, George stayed after hours and oftentimes did their jobs for them. When hard times came, and the newspaper found it necessary to let him go, his extra labor had earned for him a sum of $80. He decided to take the money and go into the business of making candy.

George's grandfather had made American candy in London and Manchester, and his father had owned the first candy machine in the territory; George was simply following in logical footsteps. Beginning with one sandstone candy slab, four iron edging bars, a candy drop machine, a pair of candy shears, some candy hooks, and a few pans, he rented a small building on Center Street and began to work.

When George finished his first batch of candy, it was a bright summer's day. As he stood back proudly to look at his work, rain began to splash

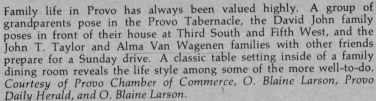

Family life in Provo has always been valued highly. A group of grandparents pose in the Provo Tabernacle, the David John family poses in front of their house at Third South and Fifth West, and the John T. Taylor and Alma Van Wagenen families with other friends prepare for a Sunday drive. A classic table setting inside of a family dining room reveals the life style among some of the more well-to-do. *Courtesy of Provo Chamber of Commerce, O. Blaine Larson, Provo Daily Herald, and O. Blaine Larson.*

through leaks in the roof and suddenly his candy was in danger. Quickly young George gathered some Adam's chewing gum, and chewing it vigorously as he crawled up to the roof, plugged the leaks to save his precious merchandise.

By 1897 his business had grown so much that he and his brother Walter built a little brick factory on Third West. In 1900 they built the large plant on First West and Sixth South near the railroad tracks. The candy company has brought employment to an average of 175 people through the years, offering the employees certain benefits and a profit-sharing bonus which was unheard of at the time. Through the panic years, the efforts of industrious men like George Startup helped return security and steadiness to the economy of the area.[11]

This Provo Fire station, built in 1892, stood at 48 East Center on the north side of Courthouse Square until it was torn down in 1923. *Courtesy of O. Blaine Larson.*

Similar stories of individual effort typify the progress in all industries. Until 1899 A. O. Smoot and Reed Smoot had been furnishing electricity for Provo in connection with the Provo Woolen Mills; however, now there was a need for a greater power plant capable of serving the entire territory. A man named L. L. Nunn, attorney for a gold mine company in Telluride, Colorado, who was interested in furnishing electrical power for mines, had experimented with alternating currents that would furnish enough power to run tramways and machinery. As the need for more power in Utah arose and Utah miners had successfully contacted him to help them with their mines, Provo citizens asked Nunn's help to establish, at the mouth of Provo Canyon, the first large plant in the United States to use alternating current. It was known as the Telluride Power Company. By 22 September 1899 the Telluride plant was in full operation. Now more electricity, available to more people, was a new signal for increased development of industry and a secure rate of growth for the area.[12]

During these difficult years Utah also buckled down to achieve statehood and finally on 4 January 1896, in a proclamation signed by Grover Cleveland, Utah became the forty-fifth state of the United States of America. In 1897, the following year, the Uinta National Forest was established. Although Utah, during the decade of the nineties, had seen insecure times with both boom and panic, the people were on a firm enough foundation to become a functioning part of the federal union.

ANDERSON-LARSON
PROVO
U.T

W.C.T.U. GO BACK TO YOUR KNITTING.
TRUTH CRUSHED TO EARTH SHALL RISE AGAIN.
ROGER WILLIAMS STILL LIVES.
Salt Lake Tribune
They are Slaves Who Dare Not be in the Right with TWO OR THREE.
Our Country IS LARGER THAN ITS RELIGIOUS BIGOTS
Frank J.
FURIOUS JUDAS CORRUPTION

SIX

CONTROVERSY AND DIVISION

The turn of the century for Provo and the surrounding area is marked by inner turmoil and controversy. As Utah accepted statehood in 1896, Mormons had to learn to accept their role as citizens in a more universal atmosphere.

Political Division

This period of adjustment was characterized mostly by political difficulties between the liberal party, or non-Mormon faction, and the People's Party, or Mormon faction. The liberals were always having to struggle for a voice. Some felt that they occasionally used trickery to get their candidates into office. For example, in 1888 territorial legislation classified the cities, making all cities over 20,000 first-class cities, those over 5,000 and less than 20,000 second-class cities, and below 5,000 third-class cities; a different set of officers were to be elected for each of these types of cities.

People had always assumed that Provo was a third-class city, and would therefore elect the roster of officers outlined for a third-class city — which included justices of the peace and aldermen. In 1890 in the city election of Provo, no count was taken of the number of citizens in the city until after four justices of the peace for the liberal party were elected. After the election, however, the People's Party took a census of Provo and discovered it to be over 5,000 in population. Therefore, they called another election which would name a mayor and ten councilmen according to the plan for second-class cities. Unhappy, the liberals, who probably had something

On 24 September 1909, Taft spoke in the Provo Tabernacle. At the podium is Reed Smoot. When the photographer, Thomas C. Larson insisted everyone hold still for the picture, Taft joked about it, saying in effect that this was the only time anybody ever told the president to keep his mouth shut. *Courtesy of O. Blaine Larson.*

to do with avoiding the count before the election, insisted on retaining two of their liberal justices of the peace as they were originally elected.[1]

In 1886 it was revealed by the newspapers of Provo that a secret society, the Loyal League of Utah, had been created in affiliation with the liberals for the purpose of keeping the state of Utah out of the Union until the Church-dominated government had been discarded. A paragraph published from the constitution of the Loyal League read:

> The objects of the Utah Loyal League are to combine the loyal people of Utah, male and female, irrespective of politics, in opposition to the political rule and the law-defying practices of the so-called Mormon Church, to oppose the admission of Utah into the Union until she has the substance as well as the form of republican government; to raise money to retain agents in Washington or elsewhere for these ends.[2]

All Utah Mormons received a lot of opposition when trying to take office in Washington, D. C. B. H. Roberts, a polygamist who was elected to Congress, was not admitted to his congressional seat. Elected from Provo to serve in the Senate, Reed Smoot — although he was monogamous — had to fight a long and hard battle for his seat. Although non-Mormons sent a document to Washington to encourage the government not to allow Smoot to take his Senate seat, Smoot went ahead with plans to serve and was sworn in. A Senate committee,

Boorey and Milliman was located on Center Street between First and Second West. *Courtesy of O. Blaine Larson.*

This large old Provo mansion still stands on Fourth South and University Avenue. *Courtesy of Dale H. Price.*

however, stopped him from taking his office. They argued that because he was a member of the Church he still believed in polygamy and was therefore not supporting the constitution or the laws of the land. A long Senate investigation of Smoot continued until February of 1907. Finally two-thirds of the Senate agreed that he was eligible and granted him his position. As a senator he served in many important capacities and gained high respect from his colleagues until he retired from office in 1932.[3]

Controversy Over Water

Not only was controversy high in the political scene, but there were inner conflicts among groups in the area who disagreed over water rights and the building of waterworks in Provo. At the turn of the

Looking southwest at the intersection of Center and Second West, the photographer has caught an interesting view of the old Methodist church. *Courtesy of O. Blaine Larson.*

The electric interurban, or Salt Lake and Utah Railroad formed by A. J. Orem, began operation in Provo in 1914, connecting with the railway to Salt Lake City. It terminated in 1946. *Courtesy of Provo Daily Herald.*

century the courts in Salt Lake City were sued for allowing the water from the Jordan Dam to flood the surrounding area. As long ago as 1864 the people of Provo and Utah County protested the desire of the Great Salt Lake Canal Company to build a dam across the Jordan River for the purpose of securing irrigation waters for the Salt Lake area. Utah County's protest helped curb the construction of the dam until the spring of 1879, when it was finally built. After this, there was always a problem with flooding and damage to Utah Valley property. Suits were in and out of courts until a low watermark was established in 1895 by both counties. The controversy concerning the waterwork situation in Provo first involved a man named Jones, who was granted a franchise to build the waterworks but forfeited it because he had demanded too much money for the use of hydrants. The Rhodes Brothers of Denver finally completed a system in 1892 using rough wooden pipes for 17 miles. But when the pipes proved to be unsatisfactory a suit was made against the brothers. Although the brothers repaired the pipes, the system still proved to be inadequate. In 1910 city bonds made possible $90,000 to improve the waterworks system.

East or West Side Depot?

These various controversies caused serious city and county problems; yet the major controversy in Provo during this time was undoubtedly the situation of the depot. This particular feud was the result of a definite division of the city into two warring

August 28, 1908.
Provo.

This depot for the electric interurban stood on the corner of First West and Center Street where J. C. Penney's now stands. *Courtesy of Provo Daily Herald.*

The old Provo roundhouse was located in the south part of town. *Courtesy of O. Blaine Larson and Nelson Wadsworth.*

factions — East against West — a situation which began early in Provo's history when the location of Main Street was on what is now Fifth West. Slowly, as the businesses built toward the east, another main street appeared on University Avenue, then "J" Street. The two railroads of the area maintained their two small depots at the south end of "J" Street. Naturally, west Provo became disturbed by its loss of business. As more and more businessmen began to choose building sites toward the east, and as the public library site was chosen on the east in 1907, there was a great deal of controversy. Feelings were not good between merchants or businessmen from either side, but real trouble began when the city wanted to build a larger depot that would serve as an adequate facility to both railroads. Provo felt that for a city of their importance they needed a better depot, but where should it be located?

The Denver and Rio Grande Western said they would build a depot if the city would grant land close to where they were now situated on University Avenue or "J" Street. However, such a move would blockade this street and prevent easy access to the other depot. Other efforts to secure land and position for the depot did not materialize either. In 1905 the Denver and Rio Grande Western said they would build a depot, and the Utah Southern Railroad thought it was a good idea and indicated that they would also use it. So an ambitious west-side businessman, T. N. Taylor, with the approval of other west Center Street businessmen, negotiated to purchase these blocks and raise money to pay for the

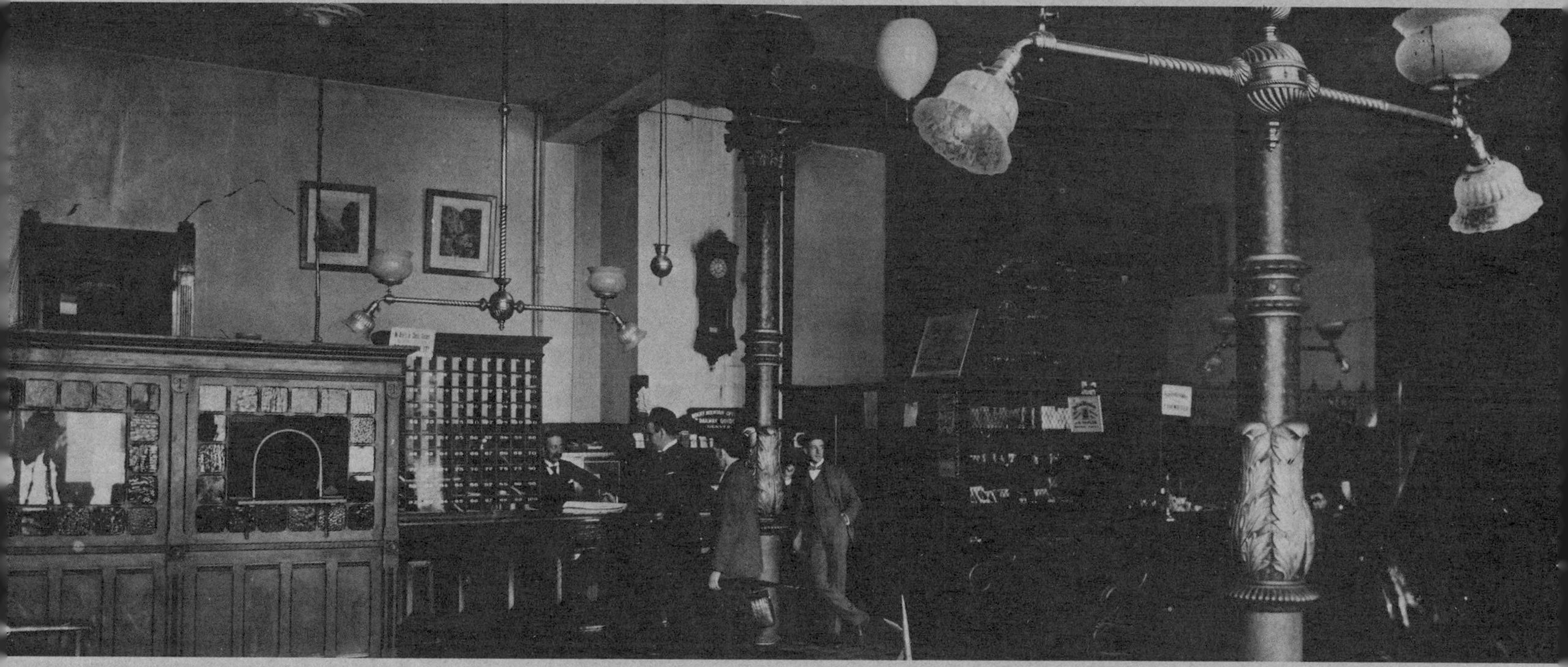

This is probably the interior of the hotel which served as one of the depots for the electric interurban. It was located where the First Security Bank now stands on First North and University Avenue. *Courtesy of O. Blaine Larson and Nelson Wadsworth.*

property. The east-end businessmen thought this action was grounds for battle, and they carried the matter over into politics. Since west-ender Joseph E. Frisby was elected mayor by a low margin of only 40 votes, he dared take no action during his two years in office to build the railroad, simply because of the bitter feelings.

Impatient to build their new depot, representatives of the railroads met with the council in April of 1908 and asked that a franchise be granted to build the railroad depot at this proposed intersection of Third West and Sixth South. In an atmosphere of bitter speeches, the franchise was denounced and action postponed. Jesse Knight secured a temporary restraining order which said that the council members could not vote for the franchise until the taxpayers voted.

For a week the taxpayers held a vigorous campaign. There were street meetings, a debate at the opera house, and bitter expressions between families and friends — those who lived on the east side and those who lived on the west. Finally, in the election on 27 July 1909, a small majority voted for the franchise to be granted to build the station in its present position, the location chosen by the west-enders.[4]

The Denver and Rio Grande did not begin working on their railroad depot until June of 1910. But on 1 January 1911 at one minute past noon, the whistles blew to announce the transfer of railroad business to a brand-new facility. Band music and speakers participated in the morning program and in the afternoon all of the officials of the railroad held a big

This Provo Cafe might have been the scene of many parties. *Courtesy of O. Blaine Larson.*

banquet at the Hotel Roberts. Both east-enders and west-enders met at these events, easing the tension caused by the disagreement.

Prohibition

Another significant controversy that raged during this period was one that was sweeping the entire nation: Prohibition. At a convention in August of 1909 the people expressed a desire for Prohibition ordinances in all the towns of Utah County. Provo's ordinance was to go into effect 1 January 1910.

Both Republican and Democratic city conventions in October approved of this ordinance. However, those who were in favor of more liberal treatment of the liquor question — or the "wets" as they were called — put on an independent ticket for the city election. After a strenuous campaign, the "wets" succeeded in electing the general officers of the city while the "dries" elected the councilmen; this action created a division in the council. The mayor and the councilmen were in direct opposition. Although the mayor urged the repeal of the Prohibition, the council refused to repeal it. When the mayor appointed a "wet" city marshal, the council would not confirm this appointment. As the council dismissed two "wet" policemen, the mayor vetoed this resolution. In the meantime, while these government officials themselves were at odds, it was very difficult to enforce Prohibition. In the next election, however, the city elected a "dry" commission, which retained and enforced the prohibition law with a unified effort, and thus met with better success.[5] The "wets"

Provo people celebrated the purchase of the lot where the BYU Maeser Building now stands. *Courtesy of Dale H. Price.*

The Provo library was completed in 1907. In the background on the right is the house that still stands today as part of the Maternity Wardrobe. *Courtesy of O. Blaine Larson.*

of Provo have never given up, however. They tried to restore the saloons in 1915 and were still trying to get liquor by the drink into the saloons of Utah in 1969.

Progress

In spite of the turmoil and controversy during this period of Provo's history, many events took place which show the progress of culture and education. In 1903 the Brigham Young Academy was named "Brigham Young University" and began offering bachelors of science and arts degrees under the presidency of George Brimhall. A new campus site was obtained during this period, and at a cost of $110,000 the Maeser memorial building was completed in 1911 in honor of Karl G. Maeser, who had died in 1901.[6] With 1,425 volumes available for public use, the Provo Library opened its doors in the courthouse on 2 January 1906. Shortly afterward, the Provo people conferred with Andrew Carnegie to receive money to develop a better building. Mr. Carnegie gave Provo City $17,500 with the agreement that Provo would contribute 10 percent of that sum annually for its maintenance. The library was built at its present location and has been remodeled and enlarged as the years passed.

Industry during the next few years saw some of its most important progress, especially in steel, iron, and machinery manufacturing businesses. In 1885 the Provo Foundry and Machine Company had established the first major industry to deal with big machinery. Although it exchanged hands several

Few remember the old iron fountain that stood for a time in the intersection of University and Center. It was constructed in 1917 at the time the city streets were paved. *Courtesy of Provo Daily Herald and John W. Bun Taylor.* Facing page: the laying of the Maeser cornerstone.

times — sometimes closing and failing, especially during hard times — by 1910, under the hand of Mr. Thomas Pierpont, it was finally shipping machinery to all parts of the world. Perhaps one of the most significant efforts of the Provo Foundry and Machine Company was its placement of a big iron fountain in the intersection of University and Center Street, a monument now visible only in some of Provo's early photographs.[7] Another foundry, the Sun Foundry, also did business during these years.

During this period the Utah Valley Iron and Manufacturing Company, which owned its own iron mines 8 miles west of Goshen, planned to bring iron across Utah and begin large production. Under the leadership of Mr. A. A. Noon the people of the area were encouraged to deal in metals on a large scale. However, although he gave lectures and wrote many newspaper articles to stimulate investments, money for the industry was difficult to come by. As a result, Mr. Noon's projects failed. However, when in 1910 a Mr. L. F. Rains from Salt Lake City saw the same possibility of metal production that Mr. Noon had seen, Rains was so enthusiastic he went to California to get money. He met with more success. Soon he laid the foundation for what was later to become the Columbia Steel Corporation at Ironton.[8]

Other businesses during this time flourished. Taylor Brothers department store, Tri-State Lumber Company, and others became well established. The Farmers and Merchants Bank was established 22 September 1906. There was the beginning also in this year of the Bingham Copper Mines and the first

LARSON
OCT=16=1909
PROVO

A group of Maeser School students celebrate. *Courtesy of O. Blaine Larson.*

A 1912 parade features the "Goddess of Liberty" in a horseless carriage surrounded by girls representing the states of the union. *Courtesy of Provo Daily Herald.*

Job's Daughters give a program. *Courtesy of O. Blaine Larson.*

This Provo First Ward basketball team won the first all-Church tournament in 1928. *Courtesy of O. Blaine Larson.*

One of Provo's most elegant homes was built by Dr. Homberg. It remains today shorn of its fancy towers at 195 South Fourth West. *Courtesy of Dale H. Price.*

On the facing page Grandfather and Grandmother Thomas C. Larson pose for a portrait with members of their large family. Their son, taking the photograph, is the Thomas C. Larson who took many of the photographs in this book. *Courtesy of O. Blaine Larson.*

The classic family self-portrait on the facing page was taken by father-photographer Thomas C. Larson. By permission of his son O. Blaine Larson, here standing at the table, we have been able to illustrate the history of Provo with many outstanding pictures. *Courtesy of O. Blaine Larson.*

SIGN WRITING
PAPER HANGING
PAINTING
SNOW & YOUNG
PAINTS OILS
BRUSHES
AND

The Provo baseball team of 1880 included on the back row: Joseph Duke, Hyrum Duke, George Dent (?) and William Halley. Seated are: George Collins, Edward Smith, Ted Smith, Nelce Markman, and Van Belvedere (?).

Alma Van Wagenen's first carriage shop was located at 310 West Center. Here he expanded to Center Street with this first shipment of Buick autos. *Courtesy of Provo Daily Herald.*

oil well at Virgin, Utah. An electric interurban line franchise was given so that an electric streetcar was built in Provo, and in 1911 J. A. Jones was given a gas franchise. Plans for Strawberry Reservoir were made, and Utah Power and Light under the stewardship of Abraham O. Smoot improved their facilities to make power possible for a larger area.

Studebaker buggy salesman Alma Van Wagenen brought automobiles into the valley before 1915. His first successful sales with the "horseless carriage" were made with Buicks. He carried Vim Trucks, Oakland and Scripps Reo cars, and the Hupmobile, but these makes did not catch on as successfully. For quite a while, he was the only auto dealer south of Salt Lake.[9] His business increased to good proportions as the automobile became more popular.

As well as in industry and business, Provo increased its facilities for recreation. In the summer of 1912, E. L. "Timpanogos" Roberts, chairman of BYU's Physical Education Department established the traditional summer "Timp Hike" by taking a group of students up to the summit.[10] Basketball was introduced to Provo Schools in 1906 and baseball became popular with the organization of a Central Utah Baseball League in 1920. Teams from surrounding areas came to play in Provo's Timpanogos Park. A swimming pool was built at North Park.

Although Provo had its share of difficulties and controversies in organizing and building the community, there was also a great deal of cooperative effort that made so many of its programs meet with success.

SEVEN

WORLD INFLUENCES: WAR, DEPRESSION

World War I

When the people of Utah finally accepted themselves as part of the larger nation and the inner turmoil and controversy had somewhat died down among them, it was time for World War I. For the world as well as for the people of Utah, there was no longer the possibility of isolation — withdrawal from the world at large. With modern transportation and communication everyone was part of a larger body, vulnerable to the same difficulties and dangers. There was no taking a back seat or cowering from national responsibilities.

Like the other Utah communities, Provo rallied to the causes of World War I with enthusiasm and patriotism. At the beginning of the school year in 1917, BYU made changes to accommodate the national emergency. President George H. Brimhall gave credit for all war effort. That fall he allowed both young men and young women to work in the fields rather than attend classes. "Food will win the war" became a popular slogan. The young people did not go back to school that fall until all of the crops had been harvested.[1]

Other war-effort activities included military training and first-aid education. Daily, the young women met in College Hall to learn the rudiments of first aid and nursing. No one knew whether or not the battlefield would reach Provo, so everyone tried to become prepared. Instead of intercollegiate athletics, group contests within the student body were initiated with military training as a part of

A barracks for the student army training corps was set up here in the halls of the Maeser building as part of the war effort. This picture is of the bicentennial of BYU just a few years after the war. *Courtesy of Provo Chamber of Commerce.*

every day's activities. Three times a week students would get out and take long marches around the countryside to build up their stamina.

Many of the young men, of course, left to serve in the military. This left the girls home to do other things. Knitting became very popular. The girls produced 174 sweaters, 50 pairs of socks, 23 shawls, 19 scarves, and three helmets. They also made clothing for Belgian infants and children: dresses, jackets, and other items. The wives of the faculty members participated in money-raising luncheons and other activities to purchase bonds. Students also appropriated money from their treasury to buy bonds. They worked part time on Saturdays, after school, and during many other hours just so they could send money to the government.

At one time the federal government decided to set up student army training corps in the universities. A corps was initiated at BYU, but there were no facilities available in which to house the training units. The women rallied to collect 300 mattresses and 900 quilts — a feat they performed in only five days. Placing them in the halls of the Maeser Building, they created a giant barracks with beds lying everywhere. At the time of the influenza epidemic, which took its toll in Provo as in other areas, the women baked bread, biscuits, cakes, and cookies for the units, and nursed them back to health.

For the commencement exercises of 1917, George H. Brimhall wrote a song called "Old Glory," which became a patriotic favorite, not only among the people of Provo, but among those men who went

These dramatic shots of the fire at the Woolen Mills in 1918 show somewhat the extent of the destruction. *Courtesy of Provo Daily Herald.* Below, Provo's fire station, 1923 to the 1960s.

overseas. Cole W. Reed, who wrote the music for the song, also wrote the "Knitting Song," which was popular for the young women who had stayed at home to tend to domestic tasks that would support the men in their fighting.[2] The ladies even rallied by organizing the "Ladies' Military Band," which was so popular it continued to play long after the war was over.

Fire at the Woolen Mills

Not only did the people of Provo Valley support the war in a united effort by preparation and by sacrifice of men and money, but they increased their industry at this time, especially at the woolen mills and in the production of steel. Although the woolen mills had encountered difficulties through the years because of

At its peak, the Ironton steel plant was one of the largest in the United States. *Courtesy of O. Blaine Larson.*

transportation costs and competing markets, they now employed a large staff, and, having been reincorporated under the ownership of Jesse Knight, were having good success. In 1914 a new cutting and sewing department had been added and a new building constructed to house it. Mackinaws, flannel shirts, and heavy blankets were now produced for markets in the colder northern states.

The mills were at their peak of productivity when, in July of 1918, just three months before the termination of World War I, disaster struck. On 30 July 1918, these words appeared in a Provo *Post* newspaper story: "With a wild cry of 'fire' Grant Eggersted, one of the employees of the Knight Woolen Mills gave the first warning cry for the worst holocaust in the history of Provo." The fire was thought to have been caused by spontaneous combustion in the wool drier. The Provo *Post* estimated the loss to be more than $500,000. From this fire, without question the greatest destruction in Provo's history, the woolen mills never fully recovered.

Steel

During World War I L. F. Rains's efforts to secure money for the steel industry in Utah Valley materialized. As a member of the Columbia Steel Corporation, Mr. Rains negotiated with California and Eastern companies to bring a plant into this area. Springville seemed most anxious to furnish a site for the industry and offered 400 acres of Springville pasture. When representatives from San Francisco

The Provo City office building on Courthouse Square was razed in 1971. A fountain now occupies that spot. *Courtesy of Provo Daily Herald.*

visited and indicated that more land was needed, Springville eagerly joined with Provo to raise $40,000 for the purchase of 600 more acres.[3] In 1923 the land was ready, and the Columbia Steel Corporation began building their operation at Ironton. On 1 May 1924 the first Utah iron was produced.

In appreciation for what Mr. L. F. Rains accomplished by bringing the industry into the area, the mayor of Salt Lake City, C. Clarence Nelson, said:

> I don't know what the initials L. F. [stand] for in his name; I have thought they stood for 'Long Foresight'; then again I have thought they stood for 'Legitimate Finance,' but after a close association with him I believe they stand for 'Loyal Friendship.'[4]

Quickly following the Ironton plant, other industries moved into the area: the Republic Creosoting Plant, the National Pump Company, and the Pacific States Cast Iron Pipe Company. A huge housing development for plant workers was mapped out on the hill just east of the Ironton operation; hundreds of dollars were spent for surveying and street planning. A few homes went up, but, as use of the automobile became more popular, people wanted to live in suburbs away from the factory and commute to their jobs. All that is left of the planned housing development are a few lots sparsely settled and some high-sounding street names, such as "California."

This picture of the St. Francis Catholic Church was taken before it was finished in 1969 with its stucco and tile reminiscent of the old California missions.

The old Provo High School stood on the block now occupied by the city center. In this photograph taken by Herald photographer Mark Rigtrup in 1963, the building is being torn down. *Courtesy of Provo Daily Herald.*

Community Church

As Provo left the years of World War I, the effects of the unifying effort seemed to stay with them. The entire spirit during the war effort had been one of unity; even the churches had pulled together at this time — especially the denominations other than Mormon. Although the Methodist, Baptist, and Congregational churches had been in the area for quite a while — the Methodists had been first in 1873, followed by the First Congregational Church in 1882, with its own school, the Proctor Academy, built in 1887, and the Baptists in 1892 — just before World War I, on 1 June 1917 these community churches decided to join hands and unite under the broad policies of the Congregationalists. In 1918, just after the war began, they incorporated under the name of Provo Community Congregational Church, and have functioned in this united way ever since.[5] The Catholics began in 1923 to construct their beautiful Italian Renaissance cathedral at this time.[6]

Community Progress

In other areas the community seemed to pull together. It was in the year of 1922 that the new County Courthouse was completed in its present location; a new fire department was organized; a golf course was laid out in 1923. A new high school was erected in 1919 and the first community airport was established in the same year. In 1924 a rousing Diamond Jubilee was held for Provo, at which a silk flag made by Provo ladies from silk grown and woven

in Provo was proudly displayed. On 26 April of that same year Provo presented a Utah County Symphony Orchestra concert under the direction of Franklin Madsen.

Provo was also proud of its baseball team during this period, and its BYU basketball and tennis teams, which both won state championships in 1925. And BYU's own sportsman, Clinton Larson, surprised everyone by winning the high jump at the inter-allied meet in Paris at the close of World War I.

Depression and WPA

It was not long, however, before the next major difficulty struck the Utah Valley area — the national depression. Provo suffered along with everyone else when banks closed, businesses and industries failed. The woolen mills had been closed by this time, failing partly because of a bad reputation. The story is told that they had sent to a California militia some blue uniforms that shrank and ran with blue dye during a parade in a rainstorm.

Although during this time many disappointed people were without jobs, and were suddenly finding themselves overcome by serious financial problems, this was the time of national government aid, and Provo, like many other communities, now found itself enjoying government financing which stimulated community improvement to a new high level. With WPA appropriations, there was increased building of new schools, bridges, waterworks, sewer systems, airports, and other projects. The government sponsored expansion in Columbia Steel and

City power and lights have always been a concern of Provoans. In the background is the Provo Foundry and machine works. *Courtesy of Provo City.*

Provo City built its own power plant only after extended court struggles to take that right from private individuals. *Courtesy of Provo City.*

also a project with Deer Creek in which many miles of pipe were laid to conduct water. There were also WPA improvements at Timpanogos Cave National Monument, which stirred interest in the Timpanogos hikes, and at the Provo boat harbor. Highways and trails were improved through Provo Canyon, Alpine Loop, and Timpanogos Cave by WPA assistance. Also with WPA assistance, 58 blocks of asphalt paving were completed in Provo in 1937. A federal grant expanded Provo's library, and government offices were moved to better buildings.[7]

City Power Plant

It was during and after the depression that the transfer of Provo's power from a private concern to its own city company became a reality. Although the transfer met with opposition from Abraham O. Smoot, son of the early stake president, and others who owned the power plant in Provo, the plan to place power in the hands of the city was thoroughly investigated.

Following Mark Anderson's election as mayor of Provo in 1936, he procured signatures of 2,383 families, or approximately 75 percent of Provo's residents, on a statement in which they agreed to take electrical energy from a municipal plant if one was established. Soon the city planned the design and supervision of such a plant and at a bond election on 14 October 1936 gave approval in the way of financial support for the project.

For many weeks the existing Utah Power and Light Company opposed the new power plant, until

Despite hard times during the depression years, Provo still managed to celebrate with colorful parades. *Courtesy of Provo Daily Herald.*

in December of 1937 the Utah Supreme Court supported the city's right to build it. Still not satisfied, the existing power company continued to cause difficulty until on 13 October 1938 the United States Supreme Court supported the Utah court decision.

Finally, in April of 1940, Provo City took over its own power company. A large celebration with refreshments and a tour through the new plant marked its new use.

Smiling through Hard Times

As a community dealing with the national war and depression, Provo did quite well, increasing its industrial development, culture, and national activities. It seems the people of Provo were not going to let hard times get them down. One of their chief enjoyments during these hard years was a Sunday excursion on the *Sho-Boat*, a 90-foot two-decked yacht which toured Utah Lake on Sundays at 4:00 p.m. — 50c for adults, and 25c for children.[8] Sunday visitors went out and toured the lake, stopping at the unusual calcium-deposited Rock Island where 25,000 California gulls nested. The warm springs on the island flow through the rocks, giving them an interesting, coarse appearance. On the upper deck of the boat people stood and watched the beautiful valley scenery for miles around. On the lower deck they held dances and parties. Through these hard times there was a strong spirit of nationalism, encouragement, and dedication to private lives.

EIGHT

PROGRESS AS A MODERN COMMUNITY

Growth in the Steel Industry

The Japanese attack on Pearl Harbor, 7 December 1941, was not only to affect the entire nation as they joined World War II but to make a significant difference in the economy of Utah Valley, for with the advent of World War II came an increased need for steel, and Utah Valley was a choice area for steel production.

As soon as the United States joined the war, the federal office of Production Management requested the U.S. Steel Corporation to submit a plan for an extensive steel operation. They felt the steel plant ought to be built in the west, but not on the Pacific Coast. So, because of its accessibility to sources of iron ore, coal, limestone, and water, and its adequate railroad facilities, the Provo area was chosen.

Although the Ironton-Columbia Steel plant was at this time producing 700 tons of iron each 24 hours, more was needed, and so construction of this second giant steel industry began. Placed on the site of the old Geneva Lake Resort built up in the boom times of the 90s, it was called the Geneva Works, United States Steel Company.

The advent of this large steel industry gave Utah new importance as an industrial center in the United States. Accompanied by rousing speeches and parades in favor of the war effort, hundreds of people began moving into the Provo area during World War II to work at the government steel plant. There was a time during this period that Provo claimed to be the West's fastest growing city.

The Kiwanis Club of Provo pose in a shot taken at the Provo Brick and Tile Company plant in October of 1921. *Courtesy of Provo Daily Herald.*

Although the government operation shut down periodically following the war, there has been an overall steady increase in the industry since its purchase in 1946 by the United States Steel Company. Today, as a fully integrated steel mill, it is one of the West's largest steel facilities, producing pig iron, coke, welded steel pipe, and hot sheets and coils. Rapidly many other industries entered the valley after World War II, including industries to accompany the production of steel, such as more foundries, welding companies, sheet metal works, machine factories, and even other steel companies, such as the Pittsburgh-Des Moines Steel Plant.

Industrial Progress

Other industries entering were in all areas of production: bricks, stone, cement, houses, printing and publishing companies, and clothing manufacturers, such as Barbizon of Utah, entering Provo in 1946, or the JoLene Company late in 1956. In 1952 the LDS Church established the Deseret Industries, which now gives 300 handicapped people jobs in refinishing old furniture, mending clothing, and reclaiming any used or second-hand items. A new Deseret Industries building on State Street, northwest of the Riverside Plaza, was built and dedicated in 1965.

Community Projects

In 1946 Provo issued 444 building permits and celebrated Utah's centennial year in 1947 with pride in community accomplishments in all areas. In 1941

Provo's friendly sanitation engineers pose beside their garbage trucks in the year 1947. *Courtesy of Provo City.*

they had completed the Deer Creek Dam and Reservoir project; the sewage had been extended; and in 1942 parking meters had been installed. In 1940 city officials determined by a survey that Provo citizens would approve of a systematic garbage and refuse disposal, and so large trucks were purchased at that time, and more modern equipment since.

Hospitals

Other community projects prior to the 1940s were successfully launched; a hospital opened in 1939 with 55 beds, 12 bassinets, and 38 physicians. This original Utah Valley Hospital was built through the efforts of the Chamber of Commerce and interested doctors who secured $250,000 from the Commonwealth Fund of New York. Provo furnished a site for the hospital and donated $90,000. On 15 July 1953, at the request of the board of directors, it was turned over to The Church of Jesus Christ of Latter-day Saints, which has added to it in 1956, 1959, and 1971 until the bed count reached 260, the number of full-time staff workers rose to 675, and the number of physicians to 116. Now available for Provo medical services are a new surgical wing and a complete well-equipped laboratory, housing departments for electrocardiograph, electroencephalograph, cytology, hematology, blood bank, biochemistry, histology, microbiology, and many other facilities.

The Utah State Hospital, begun as the "Salt Lake City Insane Asylum" in 1869, had come to Provo in 1885 as a state institution and was named "Utah

The state hospital sits at the far east end of Center Street. *Courtesy of O. Blaine Larson.*

The First Security Bank building has changed its appearance, but not its location. *Courtesy of O. Blaine Larson.*

State Mental Hospital" and in 1927 "Utah State Hospital." At first the hospital operated a home for both emotionally disturbed and feebleminded until on 14 March 1929 the Utah Legislature passed the law that created the "Utah State Training School for the Feebleminded" and the children were taken to the school established at American Fork.

The major growth of the hospital in recent years has been in its movement away from a "confining" institution to one dedicated to solving social problems and helping patients return to their homes. The "Youth Center" created in 1964 by Dr. Eugene Faux has attracted attention from other hospitals, as well as the school in connection with it, which, under the direction of Dr. Glen Brown, is a part of the Provo School District and serves as a springboard for young people to get the help they need before returning to their families and communities.

Senior Center

A center for senior citizens was made possible for Provo through a gift of land donated by Mr. and Mrs. L. J. Eldred. The plot they originally donated was the corner where the U.S. Post Office was built in 1962. The Post Office took this land, but enough money was acquired from the purchase to aid in building the Eldred Center in 1964 and 1965 on its location on Third West and Fifth North. The remainder of the funds for the Eldred Center were secured by the sale of the Utahna Gardens, also given by the Eldreds to Provo, and the Royden Hotel, given to Provo by John O. Beesley. A new addition to the

Provo High School was built in 1956. *Courtesy of Provo City.*

library was dedicated on 28 July 1939, and since that time facilities have grown to include more than 65,000 books and 125 periodicals. Air conditioning, a visual aids area, a phonograph record department, and multicopier facilities have all been improvements which have increased the value of the library in recent years.

Schools

Schools have grown rapidly in the past thirty years. Provo High School, established in 1912, was ready for a new building in 1956, but there were differing feelings over where it should be located. Superintendent of Provo Schools, J. C. Moffitt, with the help of the Provo Board of Education, secured the land where the high school now stands. Some criticized the board for wanting to build the school "out in the suburbs." It was not long, however, before Provo built around and beyond it.

Other school buildings rose up all over the city. The Joaquin and Timpanogos elementary schools were built and occupied in 1938. Grandview was built in 1948-49, and the major portion of Provost and Wasatch schools, both erected as primary unit schools, were built in 1949. The first portion of Sunset View School was built in 1959, and the main portion of Rock Canyon was built in 1964, and Edgemont in 1967.

Utah Technical College at Provo, a vocational school initiated during World War II to help train young people for the war effort, has been successful as an educational institution since 1941. Throughout

Provo has always loved parades. *Courtesy of Provo City.*

the earlier years the courses offered were only those of vocational and technical nature. Beginning in 1967 general education classes were offered. Recently added courses of study are hospital ward clerk, nurse's aide, psychiatric aide, and psychiatric technician. The latest additions to the curriculum are data processing, electromechanical technology, and X-ray technology. Plans are being made for new buildings at a larger site in southwest Orem.

Brigham Young University did most of its building under the presidency of Ernest L. Wilkinson, who left his position to Dallin Oaks in 1971 after the enrollment had catapulted to 25,000.

In 1973 the campus of the University in Provo covered in excess of 529 acres, including 33 permanent academic buildings, 47 less permanent academic buildings, 27 service buildings, 9 temporary service buildings, 41 residence halls, 588 family apartment units, 27 administrative and auxiliary service units, a dairy and poultry farm of 610 acres, and a motion picture studio with 22 acres of land.

In 1973, 1,660 employees were working at the University, with 1,137 as members of the professional teaching faculty and 38 more on temporary leave of absence.

Brigham Young University has made significant cultural contributions to the city of Provo. For over 75 years, BYU's orchestras, vocal groups, and bands have given many concerts, chamber recitals, and operas, and the bands have participated in hundreds of parades. BYU has brought to Provo the best symphonies of the world, such as the Berlin and

The BYU band shows off during fancy halftime maneuvers at a football game in the old stadium. The Richards Building now stands in this football field. *Courtesy of Provo City.*

Provoans enjoy ice skating in Utah Lake boat harbor. *Courtesy of Provo City.*

London Philharmonic orchestras.

As well as serving as the chief athletic interest in the area, with top basketball and football teams, the University has also sponsored popular track and field meets for the community at large and special band days for students of the intermountain high schools.

The influence of the Springville Art Gallery and the Harris Fine Arts Center have increased Provo's interest in visual arts. Dramatic arts also continue to flourish in the University.

City Government

As well as in educational and cultural growth, the last few decades in Provo have seen growing pains in city government. During the 1950s the city stepped out courageously to try a new form of government under a council-manager charter. Through a series of debates, Provo citizens analyzed the advantages and disadvantages and finally, in a special election on 8 August 1955, voted to change. On 3 January 1956 Harold E. Van Wagenen became mayor.

For six years Provo tried this form of government, until in 1961 Mr. Verl H. Dixon encouraged a return to the city commission plan. As he took the office of mayor in 1962, by another special election the government returned to its earlier form. The commission has had powers to administer departments in all areas of municipal improvement — the expansion of city water, streets, sidewalks, sewer extensions and disposals, curbs and gutters, parks

Provo City Center was completed in 1972. *Courtesy of Provo City.*

and recreation facilities, garbage collections, and health facilities, including sanitation.

Provo City Center

Until 1962 Provo City had been occupying office space in the Utah City-County building, which it had helped to erect back in 1926. In 1962 the city sold its interest in that building to Utah county and began looking for a new home. For approximately a decade the city offices occupied the former post office building at University Avenue and Center Street. Continuous growth required larger building facilities. After much careful committee work, it was decided that a new city building should be built on the block between Third and Fourth West, adjacent to Center Street.

On 26 June 1968, recommendation was made by the advisory committee that the new building be given the name "Provo City Center." This proposal was approved by the city commission. The city commission spent several months listening to citizens and the advisory committee pertaining to the location of the building, the proposed bonding program, and plans for the construction of the building. Many suggestions were made to the commission concerning ways by which the taxpayers may be properly informed before voting on the proposed bond issue.

By 31 July 1968, the announcement was made public that the amount of the bonds would be for $3,000,000, much of which would come from general property taxes.

The bond election for the purpose of determining

In the pioneer museum located on the site of the old Sowiette Fort are artifacts of Provo's pioneer history. *Courtesy of Provo City.*

This monument and modern replica mark the spot of the original Utah Fort. *Courtesy of Provo City.*

the willingness of the Provo taxpayers to authorize the city commission to sell general obligation bonds amounting to the needed $3,000,000 was held 20 August 1968. By vote the people decided to build the city complex, and it was completed in 1972.

For the first time in all of Provo's history, one structure could house all departments directly affiliated with city government. The completion and occupancy of this edifice by local government in downtown Provo was a new milestone in the city's history.

Service to the Community

Not only has city government played an important part in community development, but men's and women's service organizations and clubs have done a great deal to promote projects helpful to the city. The Rotary and Kiwanis organizations have helped establish parks; the Women's Council built a club building for the use of all Provo citizens. Other organizations to give help have been, for the men: Lions, Jaycees, Sertoma, Utah Lake Lions, Timpanogos Kiwanis, Exchange, Edgemont Lions, and Timpanogos Lions. The women's clubs are Business and Professional Women, Jaycees' Wives, Provo La Sertoma, Altrusa, Utah Lake Lady Lions, Edgemont Lady Lions, Federated Women, and Lady Lions.

For the beautification of Provo, more than 1,314 acres of ground were available as of 1966 for park development, with 210 of these acres in use. As the need arises, the balance of this land is slowly being

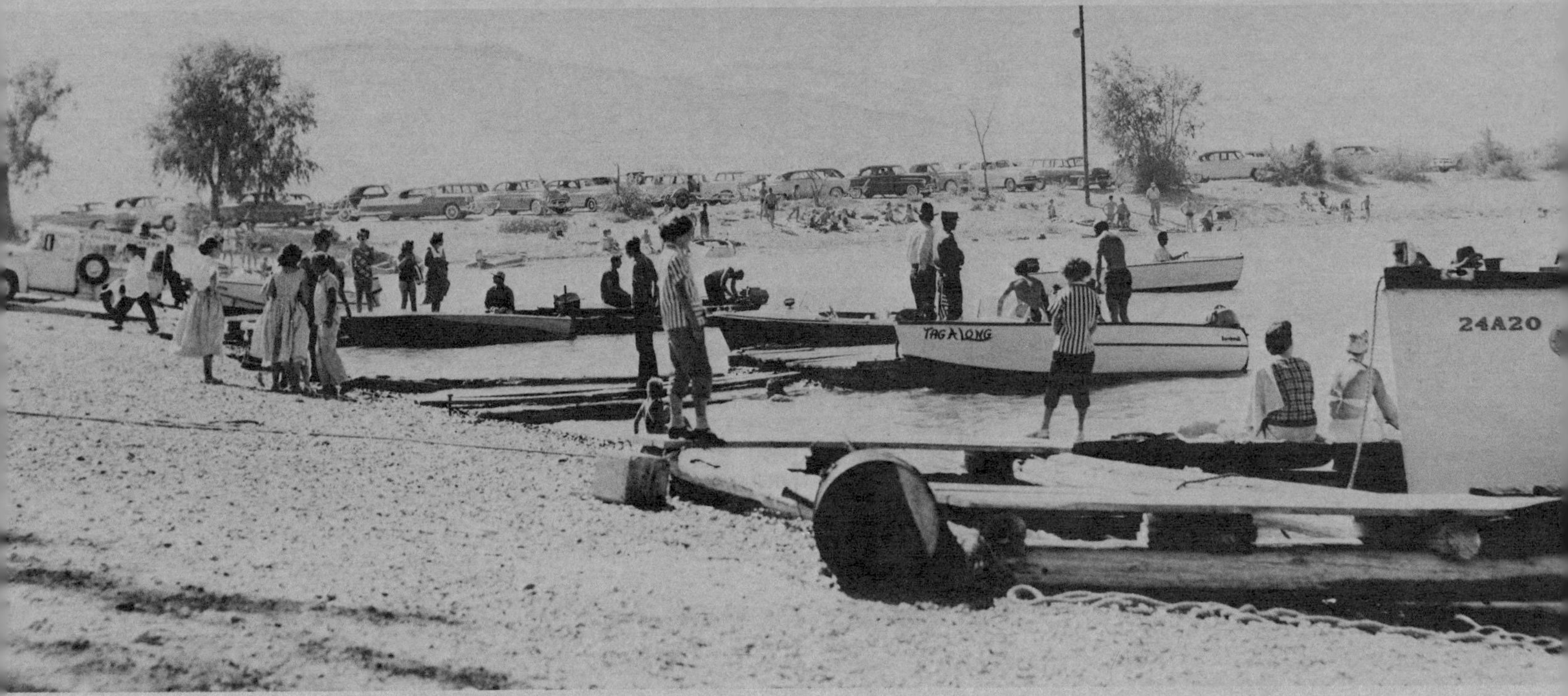

Boating on the Utah Lake has always been popular. *Courtesy of Provo City.*

developed. A master shade-tree program was established some years ago in which the city, in connection with its own nursery, removes old trees and plants new ones.

As well as parks and shady streets, Provo maintains a well-kept cemetery on South State Street. At one time in early Provo history a cemetery was established on the hill where the Maeser Building of Brigham Young University now stands. The bodies were removed from this site and placed in their present location where (it is hoped) they still lie along with all the others who have passed their way.

Among the park-recreational facilities available to Provoans and kept by the city is an excellent municipal twenty-seven-hole golf course, in addition to the private Riverside Country Club golf course and the facilities at the harbor near the spot where Provo River enters Utah Lake. Much of the work of the development of the harbor was done by Provo City in connection with the National Parks Service and the Civilian Conservation Corps.

As well as honoring the pioneers by continuing to hold extravagant July 4 and 24 celebrations complete with festivals and parades, Provo continues to support the museum in Sowiette Park in the vicinity where Chief Sowiette offered his personal defense and that of his warriors at a time when the followers of Chief Walker would have murdered them. This museum building was officially opened 5 August 1938.

Another building that still honors pioneer times is the Provo Tabernacle, still used by Provo wards for

stake conferences. Rather than tear down this historic edifice, the Provo stakes remodeled it in 1969-70.

One of Provo's most significant new buildings is the beautiful Provo Temple, built by The Church of Jesus Christ of Latter-day Saints. Ground was broken in 1969 and the temple completed in 1972. Five days a week members of the Mormon Church attend religious sessions in the temple, doing temple work. The situation of the temple up on the hill and the landscaping of the grounds have added much to the beauty of the city. The lights at night on the spire were a memorable feature until the energy crisis of 1973 demanded they be employed less frequently.

In 1972 the assessed evaluation of Provo had reached almost 53 million dollars. There were over 500 building permits issued in each of the previous years, and there were 142 miles of paved streets, 143 miles of concrete sidewalks, 165 miles of curb and gutter, 150 miles of water mains, and 102 miles of sewer lines. The city had been established as a convenient and attractive area for people to live.

From its beginning as a small fort built in a wide open valley, Provo has become an important population center of Utah, involved in national and local political and cultural activities. In the 1970s it still looks forward to growth.

Credits for Full-page Photographs

Cover. This is a picture of Provo's railroad station before the present depot was built. *Courtesy of John W. Taylor.*

Page 26. This photo was taken at Provo's railroad station at the time of Taft's visit in 1909. *Courtesy of Provo Daily Herald.*

Page 33. A Provo industry. *Courtesy of O. Blaine Larson and Nelson Wadsworth.*

Page 40. Utah Lake served not only as a resort, but supported a fishing industry for many years. *Courtesy of O. Blaine Larson.*

Page 45. Early photographer G. E. Anderson captured a classic pose of the winning Provo boat crew of 1890. *Courtesy of Rell G. Francis.*

Page 51. This photograph records an early celebration at the Brigham Young Academy Building. *Courtesy of Provo Chamber of Commerce.*

Page 55. A horse fair. *Courtesy of O. Blaine Larson.*

Page 56. This political campaign was typical of many which took place in Courthouse Square. In the background on the left are the jail and stray pen situated along First East. In the back, the fence on the right runs along First South. *Courtesy of O. Blaine Larson.*

Page 67. This photograph shows the laying of the Maeser Building cornerstone 16 October 1909. White-bearded President Joseph F. Smith officiated at the ceremonies. Reed Smoot stands to the left. *Courtesy of O. Blaine Larson.*

Page 68. This horse fair was held in Courthouse Square. *Courtesy of Provo Chamber of Commerce.*

Page 74. A Provo business. *Courtesy of O. Blaine Larson and Nelson Wadsworth.*

Page 76. Provo holds a rally in front of the courthouse prior to the departure of men who were to fight in World War I. *Courtesy of O. Blaine Larson.*

Page 86. Geneva Steel plant. *Courtesy of Provo Chamber of Commerce.*

NOTES

Chapter 1

1. Workers of the Writers' Program of the Work Projects Administration, comps., *Provo: Pioneer Mormon City*, American Guide Series (Portland: Binfords and Mort, 1942), p. 36; hereafter cited as WPA.
2. WPA, p. 37.
3. J. Marinus Jensen, *History of Provo, Utah* (Provo: J. Marinus Jensen, 1924), p. 17.
4. WPA, p. 21.
5. Jensen, *History of Provo*, p. 29.

Chapter 2

1. WPA, p. 38.
2. WPA, p. 44.
3. WPA, p. 45.
4. Hubert Howe Bancroft, *History of Utah* (San Francisco: The History Co., 1890), p. 309.
5. WPA, p. 49.
6. WPA, p. 53.
7. Jensen, *History of Provo*, p. 46.
8. WPA, p. 59.
9. WPA, p. 67.
10. Jensen, *History of Provo*, p. 391.
11. WPA, p. 75.
12. WPA, pp. 79-80.

Chapter 3

1. WPA, pp. 83-84.
2. WPA, p. 84.
3. WPA, p. 87.
4. Gustive O. Larson, *Outline History of Territorial Utah* (Provo: Brigham Young University Press), p. 96.
5. WPA, p. 89.
6. WPA, p. 90.
7. WPA, p. 92.
8. WPA, p. 95.
9. Jensen, *History of Provo*, p. 338.
10. *Deseret News*, 5 September 1860.
11. Jensen, *History of Provo*, p. 169.

Chapter 4

1. Jensen, *History of Provo*, p. 306.
2. Mary Lee Smoot and Samuel P. Smoot, comps., Smoot Family Journal, (Dallas, 1964), in possession of Mike Kawasaki, Provo, Utah.
3. Jensen, *History of Provo*, p. 309.
4. WPA, p. 123.
5. Jensen, *History of Provo*, p. 342.
6. Jensen, *History of Provo*, pp. 399-404.
7. Smoot, Smoot Family Journal.

Chapter 5

1. Jensen, *History of Provo*, p. 329.
2. Jensen, *History of Provo*, pp. 378-80.
3. WPA, p. 132.
4. WPA, p. 132.
5. Jensen, *History of Provo*, p. 267.
6. Jensen, *History of Provo*, p. 397.
7. Jensen, *History of Provo*, pp. 193-94.
8. Jensen, *History of Provo*, p. 331.
9. Jensen, *History of Provo*, p. 332.
10. Jensen, *History of Provo*, p. 333.
11. Jensen, *History of Provo*, p. 283.
12. WPA, pp. 140-41.

Chapter 6

1. Jensen, *History of Provo*, pp. 194-95.
2. Jensen, *History of Provo*, p. 189.
3. WPA, p. 112.
4. Jensen, *History of Provo*, pp. 335-37.
5. Jensen, *History of Provo*, p. 219.
6. WPA, p. 156.
7. WPA, p. 119.
8. Jensen, *History of Provo*, p. 293.
9. *Provo Herald*, 5 August 1973.
10. Jensen, *History of Provo*, p. 358.

Chapter 7

1. Jensen, *History of Provo*, p. 362.
2. Jensen, *History of Provo*, p. 364.
3. Jensen, *History of Provo*, p. 295.
4. Jensen, *History of Provo*, pp. 299-300.
5. Jensen, *History of Provo*, p. 373.
6. Jensen, *History of Provo*, p. 375.
7. WPA, p. 138.
8. WPA, p. 159.

APPENDIX

Utah Stake Tabernacle Choir, 1902

Bottom row, left to right: Elizabeth Borden, Hattie Elliott, Maud Boshard, Ida Boshard, Miss Pike, J. R. Boshard, Viola Barney, Minnie Hathenbrook, Jennie Buckley, Alice Noyes, Stella Gray. *Second row:*

Fern Cluff, Jennie Worsley, John W. Baker, Miss Cluff, Elsie Ashworth, Emma John, Etta Farrer, Reed Strong, Rhoda Douglas, Reed Boshard, William Boshard. *Third row:* Percy Burles, John Johnson, Sara Douglas, Emma Choules, Roxey Cluff, Harry Boshard, Alfred Worsley, Nome Beck, Kate Burles. *Fourth row:* Maud Cluff, Orson Bird, Ada Wardell, Walter Whitehead, Julia Ramsey, Milley Peters, Stella Thomas, Flora Cluff, Anna Douglas, George Burles, Martha Stubbs. *Fifth row:* Herbert Pyne, Clark Newell, Anna Hall, Jesse Smith, Jennie Thomas, Eugene Jones, Alice Hathenbrook, William Knudsen, Miss Twelves, Albert Choules.

Brigham Young Academy Faculty, 1891-92

Front row, from the left: Amy Brown (Lyman), Ottilie Maeser, and Mary Lyman (Cowans). *Second row:* George H. Brimhall, Emil Maeser, Nels L. Nelson, Dr. Karl G. Maeser, Emil B. Isgreen, Lars E. Eggertsen, and Hyrum Anderson. *Back row:* John E. Booth, Ephraim Gowans, Dr. Milton Hardy, Benjamin Cluff, Wilson H. Dusenberry, E. A. Wilson, and Alfred Lewis Booth.

Businesses, 1921-71

In January of 1971 the following list was compiled including all businesses that had existed in Provo for fifty years or longer.

Ahlander's Hardware and Manufacturing (J. W. Ahlander's)
American Railway Express
Anderson's (Anderson's Garage)
Ashworth Architects
Bee Hardware
Beesley Monument and Vault (Beesley Marble and Granite Works)
Bennett's Paint and Glass
Berg Mortuary (O. H. Berg and Son)
Carpenter Seed
Central Bank and Trust (State Bank of Provo)
Craghead Plumbing and Heating
The Daily Herald (Provo Herald)
Denver and Rio Grande Western Railroad
Dixon Real Estate Company
First Security Bank (Knight Trust and Savings)
Givan Ford
Hansen Candy (Hansen Catering Co.)
Heal Realty (Garden City Real Estate)
Hotel Roberts
J. C. Penney
Joseph Nelson Architect
Mortensen Plumbing (Mortensen and Son)
Mountain Bell (Mountain States Telephone and Telegraph)
Naylor Auto
P. L. Larsen Plumbing
Provo Bakery
Provo Floral (Provo Greenhouse)
Provo Savings and Loan Association (Provo Building and Loan)
Speckart's Market (Sanitary Market)
Startup Candy
Taylor's Inc. (Taylor Brothers)
Thorn Construction
Union Pacific Railroad (Los Angeles Salt Lake Railroad)
Utah Timber and Coal
Walker Bank and Trust (Farmers' and Merchants' Bank)
Western Union Telegraph

Chamber of Commerce Presidents, 1921-73

1921	Thomas A. Pierpont	1950	Max Berg
1923	John S. Smith	1951	Arch Madsen
1924	A. N. Taylor	1952	Henry D. Taylor
1925	Oscar A. Spear	1953	J. Hamilton Calder
1926	J. William Knight	1954	Paul Gehring
1928	Clayton Jenkins	1956	Arthur Adamson
1929	John O. Beesley	1957	Max Elliott
1930	L. W. Nims	1958	Robert Leishman
1931	H. Aldous Dixon	1959	Harvey Glade
1932	W. R. Butler	1960	Philip Pearlman
1934	Alex Hedquist	1961	S. E. Jacobsen
1935	I. E. Brockbank	1962	O. S. Allen
1936	J. N. Ellertson	1963	LeRoy Johnson
1937	Sidney Russell	1964	Max Hansen
1939	Frank J. Earl	1965	Dr. Lloyd Cullimore
1940	J. C. Moffitt	1967	Jack Craghead
1941	Howard Graham	1968	Dr. Wendell Vance
1942	Victor Bird	1969	Dell Ashworth
1944	P. E. Ashton	1970	Wilson Sorensen
1945	Clifton Tolboe	1971	Stan Collins
1947	F. V. Nichols	1972	Gordon Bullock
1948	Aura Hatch	1973	Glen Thomas

City Government

Under a charter granted by the General Assembly of the State of Deseret, approved 6 February 1851, the subsequent officers were elected for city government throughout the years.

1851-52
Mayor: Ellis Eames.
Aldermen: William Pace, Harlow Redfield, David Canfield, Samuel Clark.
Councilors: Gilbert Haws, James R. Ivie, William M. Wall, Chauncey Turner, George A. Smith, Jonathan O. Duke, David Cluff, Ross R. Rogers, Thomas G. Wilson.

1853-54
Mayor: Evan M. Green.
Aldermen: Jonathan O. Duke, Harlow Redfield, James R. Ivie, Elijah Billingsly.
Councilors: Robert T. Thomas, Miles Weaver, David Canfield, Edson Barney, Samuel Clark, Alanson Norton, James Bird, Jehu Blackburn, William F. Carter.

1855-56
Mayor: Benjamin K. Bullock.
Aldermen: Aaron M. York, Lewis Zabriskie, William P. Goddard, William A. Follett, Philander Colton.[1]
Councilors: Anson P. Winsor, Elisha Jones, David E. Bunnell, Lewis C. Zabriskie, John H. Carter, Alfred D. Young, Lewis O. Glazier, William F. Carter, James Bird.
1. Appointed vice William A. Follett, resigned.

1857-58
Mayor: Benjamin K. Bullock.
Aldermen: Aaron M. York, Lewis Zabriskie, William A. Follett, William O. Sperry.
Councilors: Anson P. Winsor, Elisha Jones, David E. Bunnell, Lewis C. Zabriskie, Alfred D. Young, John H. Carter, Lewis O. Glazier, William F. Carter, James Bird.

1859-60
Mayor: Benjamin K. Bullock.
Aldermen: Isaac Higbee, David E. Bunnell, John Riggs, Moses Jones.
Councilors: William O. Sperry, John H. Carter, Abram G. Cownover, Harvey H. Clubb, Elisha Jones, James Bird, Edward W. Clark,[1] Joseph Clark, Assa B. York, Sydney R. Carter.
1. Appointed vice Elisha Jones, resigned.

1861-62
Mayors: Ebenezer Hanks, Andrew H. Scott.[1]
Aldermen: Robert T. Thomas, Abram G. Cownover, Alanson Norton, Edward W. Clark,[2] George W. Bean.
Councilors: Isaac Bullock, Howard Coray, Benjamin M. Roberts, William B. Pace, L. John Nuttall, Myron Tanner, Elliott A. Newell, William A. Follett, John W. Turner.
1. Appointed vice Ebenezer Hanks, resigned.
2. Appointed vice Alanson Norton, resigned.

1863-64
Mayors[1]: Isaac Bullock, Benjamin K. Bullock.[2]
Aldermen: Robert T. Thomas, Benjamin K. Bullock, William E. Nuttall.[3]
Councilors: John H. Carter, James W. Loveless, Harvey H. Cluff.
1. By act of the governor and legislative assembly, approved 16 January 1862, the council was reduced to one mayor, two aldermen and three councilors.
2. Appointed vice Isaac Bullock, resigned.
3. Appointed vice B. K. Bullock, resigned.

1864-65
Mayor: William Miller.[1]
Aldermen: John Leetham, William E. Nuttall, L. John Nuttall,[2] David Cluff, Jr.
Councilors: James E. Daniels, James W. Loveless, Benjamin K. Bullock, Alexander F. MacDonald, Harvey H. Cluff.
1. By an act approved 21 January 1964, the present city charter was established authorizing one mayor and at least three aldermen and five councilors.
2. Appointed vice William E. Nuttall, resigned.

1866-67
Mayor: William Miller.
Aldermen: Myron Tanner, James E. Daniels, James W. Loveless.
Councilors: L. John Nuttall, John P. R. Johnson, William B. Pace, Samuel S. Jones, Warren N. Dusenberry, George M. Brown.[1]
1. Appointed vice Warren N. Dusenberry, resigned.

1868-69
Mayor: Abraham O. Smoot.
Aldermen: Elijah F. Sheets, William Miller, Myron Tanner.
Councilors: Wilford Woodruff, Joseph F. Smith, Alexander F. MacDonald, George G. Bywater, David Cluff, Jr.

1870-71
Mayor: Abraham O. Smoot.
Aldermen: William Miller, Myron Tanner, Elijah F. Sheets.
Councilors: Isaac Bullock, Warren N. Dusenberry, Alexander F. MacDonald, John P. R. Johnson, Alexander Gillespie.

1872-73
Mayor: Abraham O. Smoot.
Aldermen: Myron Tanner, L. John Nuttall, John B. Milner.
Councilors: Isaac Bullock, Warren N. Dusenberry, Alexander F. MacDonald, John P. R. Johnson, William B. Pace, Wilson H. Dusenberry.[1]
1. Appointed vice Alexander F. MacDonald, resigned.

1874-75
Mayor: Abraham O. Smoot.
Aldermen: L. John Nuttall, Wilson H. Dusenberry,[1] Albert Jones, Samuel S. Jones.
Councilors: James Dunn, William B. Pace, William A. Follett, John B. Milner, James W. Loveless, John E. Booth.[2]
1. Appointed vice L. J. Nuttall, resigned.
2. Appointed vice John B. Milner, resigned.

1876-77
Mayor: Abraham O. Smoot.[1]
Aldermen: Wilson H. Dusenberry, Albert Jones, Myron Tanner, Henry C. Rogers, John E. Booth.[2]
Councilors: William B. Pace, Harvey H. Cluff, Ole H. Berg, Warren N. Dusenberry, James W. Loveless, George Taylor, Peter M. Wentz, William J. Lewis.
1. By an ordinance passed 18 January 1877 the number of aldermen was increased to four and the number of councilors to eight.
2. Elected vice Henry C. Rogers, resigned.

1878-79
Mayor: A. O. Smoot.
Aldermen: Wilson H. Dusenberry, Isaac Bullock, Myron Tanner, John E. Booth.
Councilors: Ole H. Berg, Roger Farrer, Jr., James W. Loveless, Albert Jones, W. D. Roberts,[1] Peter Madsen, V. L. Halliday,[2] Peter M. Wentz.
1. Appointed vice Henry A. Dixon, resigned.
2. Appointed vice George M. Brown, resigned.

1880-81
Mayor: A. O. Smoot.
Aldermen: W. H. Dusenberry, Isaac Bullock, Myron Tanner, John E. Booth.
Councilors: Thomas Allman, J. P. R. Johnson, James W. Loveless, Albert Jones, Frank Scott, W. D. Roberts, A. D. Holdaway,[1] Andrew Watson.
1. Appointed vice John Meldrum, resigned.

1882-83
Mayor: Wilson H. Dusenberry.
Aldermen: S. S. Jones, James Dunn,[1] Myron Tanner, A. D. Holdaway.[2]
Councilors: J. P. R. Johnson, Roger Farrer, Jr.,[3] J. C. Graham,[4] Walter Scott,[5] David Holdaway, M. P. Madsen, Joseph T. McEwan,[6] P. M. Wentz.
1. Appointed vice Isaac Bullock, resigned.
2. Appointed vice John E. Booth, resigned.
3. Appointed vice James E. Daniels, resigned.
4. Appointed vice James W. Loveless, resigned.
5. Appointed vice R. C. Kirkwood, resigned.
6. Appointed vice A. D. Holdaway, resigned.

1884-85
Mayor: Wilson H. Dusenberry.
Aldermen: A. O. Smoot, Jr., Walter Scott,[1] W. D. Roberts, A. D. Holdaway.
Councilors: Robert Farrer, Jr., Niels Johnson, A. G. Cownover, W. A. McCullough,[2] William H. Brown,[3] David Holdaway, P. M. Wentz, Joseph T. McEwan.
1. Appointed vice James Dunn, resigned.
2. Appointed vice Walter Scott, resigned.
3. Appointed vice Mads P. Madsen, resigned.

1886-87
Mayor: Wilson H. Dusenberry.
Alderman: A. O. Smoot, Jr. Walter Scott, William H. Brown, John E. Booth.
Councilors: C. D. Glazier, Roger Farrer, Jr., Evan Wride, Wm. A. McCullough, David Holdaway, John M. Holdaway, James A. Bean, Joseph T. McEwan.

1888-89
Mayor: Wilson H. Dusenberry.
Aldermen: W. D. Alexander, James Dunn, John A. Brown,[1] Amos D. Holdaway.
Councilors: Roger Farrer, Jr., James E. Daniels, Jorgan Hansen, W. R. H. Paxman, James E. Talmage,[2] David Holdaway,[3] James A. Bean, Henry J. Maiben.
1. Appointed vice B. W. Briggs, Jr., and James Talmage, resigned respectively.
2. Appointed vice John A. Brown, resigned.
3. Resigned and appointed alderman; office of councilor remained vacant.

1890-91
Mayor: John E. Booth.
Councilmen: R. H. Thomas, L. S. Glazier, E. C. Henrichsen, James F. Dunn, Samuel Liddiard, Henry J. Maiben, John D. Dixon.

1892-93
By statute the offices of aldermen and one councilor were abolished.
Mayor: Warren N. Dusenberry.
Councilmen: Roger Farrer, Jr., Royal Barney,[1] William A. McCullough, Julius Hannberg, Abraham Halladay, William S. Holdaway, F. H. Simmons, E. A. Wilson,[2] R. R. Irvine, Joseph T. McEwan.[3]
1. Appointed President of Council. See Chapter 18, Sec. 2, Laws of Utah, 1892.
2. Appointed vice William Probert, resigned.
3. Appointed vice Henry J. Maiben, resigned.

1894-95
Mayor: Lafayette Holbrook.
Councilmen: Josiah W. Cluff, Richard Brereton, E. J. Ward, Andrew Knudsen, Abraham Halladay, Nephi Ross, F. H. Simmons, John W. Hoover, Jr., Joseph T. McEwan, Ben R. Eldredge, J. N. Strong,[1] C. D. Glazier,[2] Wm. S. Holdaway,[3] Joseph B. Keeler.[4]
1. Appointed vice Josiah W. Cluff, died.
2. Appointed vice Richard Brereton, resigned.
3. Appointed vice Nephi Ross, resigned.
4. Appointed vice Ben R. Eldredge, resigned.

1896-97
Mayor: Lafayette Holbrook.
Councilmen: Roger Farrer, Thomas Beesley, D. R. Beebe, H. J. W. Goddard, George T. Peay, Myron Tanner, William J. Lewis, Thomas Martin, Myron C. Newell, H. B. Smart.

1898-99
Mayor: S. S. Jones.
Councilmen: Thomas Beesley, Brig Johnson, H. J. W. Goddard, W. H. Brereton, Edward V. Vincent, Alfred W. Harding, John E. Booth, Thomas Martin, Joseph B. Keeler, W. M. McKendrick, D. R. Beebe,[1] Wm. J. Lewis,[2] George S. Taylor.[3]
1. Appointed vice Brig Johnson, resigned.
2. Appointed vice J. E. Booth, resigned.
3. Appointed vice W. McKendrick, resigned.

1900-01
Mayor: Thomas N. Taylor.
Councilmen: C. E. Loose, D. R. Beebe, Alex Wilkins, James Gray, Canby Scott, L. L. Nelson, George Powelson, Albert M. Carter, George S. Taylor, John H. McEwan, Niels Johnson.[1]
1. Appointed vice C. E. Loose, resigned.

1902-03
Mayor: Thomas N. Taylor.
Councilmen: J. T. Farrer, C. F. Decker, Alex Wilkins, W. D. Roberts, Jr., W. K. Farrer, W. P. Silver, Albert M. Carter, George Powelson, John H. McEwan, George S. Taylor, Joseph Ward.[1]
1. Appointed vice John F. Van Wagenen, resigned.

1904-05
Mayor: William M. Roylance.
Four-year term: Niels Johnson, James Gray, Jesse Harding, Alfred L. Booth, Ernest D. Partridge.
Two-year term: Charles F. Decker, William D. Roberts, Jr., Charles H. Miller, Joseph B. Richmond, Moroni Snow.

1906-07
Mayor: Joseph H. Frisby.
Councilmen: Niels Johnson, Wilford Giles, James Gray, Ralph Poulton, Andrew Knudsen,[1] Jesse Harding, John E. Bott,[2] Charles H. Miller, Alfred L. Booth, George Powelson, Ernest D. Partridge, Moroni Snow, Jacob Evans,[3] John Van Wagenen.[4]
1. Appointed vice Ralph Poulton, resigned.
2. Appointed vice Jesse Harding, resigned.
3. Appointed vice Ernest D. Partridge, resigned.
4. Appointed vice Moroni Snow, resigned.

1908-09
Mayor: Charles F. Decker.
Councilmen: Wilford F. Giles, Hyrum F. Thomas, Andrew Knudsen, Angus G. Beebe, Charles H. Miller, James M. Jensen, George Powelson, Albert M. Carter, Myron C. Newell, John F. Van Wagenen, John J. Craner.[1]

1. Appointed vice John F. Van Wagenen, resigned.

1910-11
The following were elected in November, 1909:
Mayor: William H. Ray.
Councilmen: John E. Bott, William McCullough, Alfred W. Harding, George Powelson, Edwin S. Hinckley.
The following councilmen continued in office: Hyrum F. Thomas, Angus G. Beebe, James M. Jensen, Albert M. Carter, and Myron C. Newell.
By virtue of a law passed at the legislative session of 1911, the government of cities of the second class was vested in a mayor and two commissioners, to be known as the board of commissioners.
Commissioners: Charles Hopkins, Walter Whitehead.

1912-13
Mayor: Charles F. Decker.
Commissioners: Henry J. W. Goddard, LeRoy Dixon.

1914-15
Mayor: Charles F. Decker.
Commissioners: Henry J. W. Goddard, LeRoy Dixon.

1916-17
Mayor: James E. Daniels
Commissioners: Henry J. W. Goddard, LeRoy Dixon.

1918-19
Mayor: LeRoy Dixon.
Commissioners: Henry J. W. Goddard, Thomas C. Thompson.

1920-21
Mayor: LeRoy Dixon.
Commissioners: Thomas C. Thompson, Charles Hopkins.

1922-23
Mayor: O. K. Hansen.
Commissioners: Charles Hopkins, George P. Billings.

1924-25
Mayor: O. K. Hansen.
Commissioners: Charles Hopkins, George P. Billings.

1926-27
Mayor: O. K. Hansen.
Commissioners: Charles Hopkins, J. Elmer Jacobsen.

1928-29
Mayor: Alma Van Wagenen.
Commissioners: Charles Hopkins, J. Elmer Jacobsen.

1930-31
Mayor: Jesse N. Ellertson.
Commissioners: Charles Hopkins, Walter Whitehead.

1932-33
Mayor: Jesse N. Ellertson.
Commissioners: J. E. Snyder, Walter P. Whitehead.

1934-35
Mayor: A. O. Smoot.
Commissioners: J. E. Snyder, Walter P. Whitehead.

1936-37
Mayor: Mark Anderson.
Commissioners: Walter P. Whitehead, J. P. McGuire.

1938-39
Mayor: Mark Anderson.
Commissioners: J. P. McGuire, Jesse Haws.

1940-41
Mayor: Mark Anderson.
Commissioners: J. P. McGuire, Jesse Haws died 22 October 1940, Maurice Harding appointed to finish out the term of Commissioner Haws.
28 August 1941, Mayor Anderson resigned.
28 August 1941, Commissioner Harding resigned.
28 August 1941, Clarence H. Harmon was appointed Commissioner to finish term of Maurice Harding.
28 August 1941, Maurice Harding appointed Mayor to finish term of Mark Anderson.

1942-43
Mayor: Maurice Harding.
Commissioners: J. P. McGuire, J. H. Swapp.

1944-45
Mayor: Maurice Harding.
Commissioners: J. H. Swapp, B. D. Palfreyman.

1946-47
Mayor: Mark Anderson.
Commissioners: B. D. Palfreyman, J. Earl Lewis.

1948-49
Mayor: George E. Collard.
Commissioners: J. Earl Lewis, Eldon W. Payne.

1950-53
Mayor: C. W. Love.
Commissioners: Eldon W. Payne, Frank T. Gardner.

1954-55
Mayor: Aura G. Hatch.
Commissioners: Eldon W. Payne, W. S. Brimhall.
Effective 1 January 1956 Provo City operated under a council-manager charter.

From 1956 to 1962, officers were as follows:

1956
Mayor: Harold E. Van Wagenen.
Councilmen: Frank Killpack, George E. Collard, Marion Hinckley, Stella H. Oaks, Roy Passey, Philip Perlman.

1957
Mayor: Harold E. Van Wagenen.
Councilmen: Frank Killpack, W. Smoot Brimhall, Marion Hinckley, Stella H. Oaks, Roy Passey, Philip Perlman.

1958
Mayor: G. Marion Hinckley.
Councilmen: Stella Oaks, W. Smoot Brimhall, Roy Passey, Frank Killpack, A. K. Breinholt, Lloyd L. Cullimore.

1959
Mayor: Lloyd L. Cullimore.
Councilmen: Stella Oaks, A. K. Breinholt, W. Smoot Brimhall, N. Halvor Madsen, W. Frank Killpack, Roy Passey.

1960
Mayor: Lloyd L. Cullimore.
Councilmen: Stella Oaks, A. K. Breinholt, Ariel S. Ballif, N. Halvor Madsen, W. Frank Killpack, Roy Passey.

1961
Mayor: Ariel S. Ballif.
Councilmen: W. Frank Killpack, Sanford M. Bingham, Ronald O. Boulter, N. Halvor Madsen, Arthur R. Morin, Roy Passey.

With repeal of the council-manager charter in 1962, the city returned to the commission form of government with officers as follows:

1962
Mayor: Verl G. Dixon
Commissioners: W. Smoot Brimhall, Luke Clegg.

1965
Mayor: Verl G. Dixon.
Commissioners: W. Smoot Brimhall (7 months), LeRoy Johnson (5 months), Luke Clegg.

1966
Mayor: Verl G. Dixon.
Commissioners: Luke Clegg, Ray Murdock.

1968
Mayor: Verl G. Dixon.
Commissioners: Ray Murdock, Leo Allen.

1970
Mayor: Verl G. Dixon.
Commissioners: Russell D. Grange, Ray Murdock.

1972
Mayor: Russell D. Grange.
Commissioners: Wayne Hillier, Odell E. Miner.

Provo Banks

1881 The First National Bank, President A. O. Smoot.
1890 The Provo Commercial and Savings Bank, President Reed Smoot.
1902 The State Bank of Provo (merged into the Central Bank and Trust Company), President W. H. Ray.
1906 The Farmers' and Merchants' Bank (later became the Walker Bank and Trust Company), President Thomas W. Taylor; 1955, President Alex Hedquist.
1915 The Knight Trust and Savings Bank (later became the First Security Bank of Utah N.A.), President Jesse Knight.
1963 The Utah National Bank (later merged into Zions First National Bank), President Joseph Smith (Leon Frazier, Chairman of the Board).

Branch banks in Provo more recently have been established by Zions First National Bank, Walker Bank, First Security Bank, and Central Bank.

Superintendents of Schools

County Superintendents of Schools, Utah County
1860 Charles D. Evans
1867 Isaac Bullock
1869 David John
1872 W. H. Dusenberry
1879 M. H. Hardy
1883 George H. Brimhall
1887 M. H. Hardy
1889 E. A. Wilson

Provo City Superintendents of Schools
1890 E. A. Wilson
1893 W. S. Rawlins
1910 L. E. Eggertson
1920 H. Aldous Dixon
1924 H. Claude Lewis
1928 Charles A. Smith
1932 H. Aldous Dixon
1937 J. C. Moffitt
1964 Sherman Wing

Schools in Provo 1850-1968

1850 A log schoolhouse was constructed in the new fort.
1851 November. "Schoolhouses [including Provo] have been erected . . . and schools have been in operation the present season." Brigham Young in an epistle to the Church.
1852 November. "Many wards [including Provo] have built commodious and comfortable school buildings." *Deseret News.*
1857 "Each ward throughout the territory has provided one or more comfortable schoolhouses." Brigham Young, Message to the Legislative Assembly.
1860 October 20. "Several commodious school rooms are in course of construction in the city of Provo." Charles D. Evans, County Superintendent.
1862 First Ward schoolhouse. School taught by Warren N. Dusenberry, first principal of Timpanogos branch of the University of Deseret.
1865 "Many schoolhouses are being built from year to year." Territorial School Report.
1860 Little distinction between school buildings and church buildings.
1890 Well-established school buildings: Central School, East School, West School, North School No. 19, Far North School.

1900 Page School.
1900 Lincoln School, occupied in 1907.
1892 November 15. Board of Education renamed the schools: New Northwest School became Timpanogos; East School became Webster; Central School became Parker; West School became Franklin; No. 19 became Page School; Far North School became Mountain School.
1892 Old Timpanogos School was built.
1898 November 9. The first portion of Maeser School was completed.
1900 The old portion of Franklin School was occupied.
1908 August 31. Parker School was completed.
1909 The first portion of Central School was completed. This became a building later occupied by high school pupils.
1920 June 17. The main portion of former Provo High School was completed.
1927 The Science and Arts building on the former high school plant was erected.
1930 The Franklin Elementary School was greatly enlarged.
1931 The first section of Dixon Junior High School was completed and occupied.
1931 The first section of Farrer Junior High School was completed and occupied.
1931 The Junior High School as a separate school was first established in Provo.
1938 The Joaquin Elementary School was built.
1938 The Timpanogos Elementary School was built.
1949 The Grandview Elementary School was completed and occupied.
1949 The first portion of Provost School was built and occupied.
1949 The first unit of Wasatch School was completed and occupied.
1949 A Dixon Junior High School addition was completed.
1956 The Provo High School main building was completed and occupied.
1959 The Sunset View Elementary School was erected.
1960 A Farrer Junior High School addition was completed.
1964 A Provost addition was completed.
1964 A Dixon Junior High School addition was completed.
1964 The major portion of Rock Canyon Elementary School was completed.
1965 The Board of Education office building was erected.
1968 The Edgemont Elementary School was acquired and enlarged.

Principals of Provo Schools Since 1890

Edgemont Elementary
1967 Glen R. Brown
1968 Ray Warner
1969 Grady Edenfield

Franklin School
Still as West School:
1890 J. B. Walton
1891 W. W. Billings

As Franklin School
1894 S. P. Eggertson
1901 J. M. Jensen
1911 S. P. Eggertson
1917 George Powelson
1923 Byron Jones
1925 E. L. Fieldsted
1927 John F. Mower
1931 Emil K. Nielson
1950 Ross Backman
1951 Emil K. Nielson
1965 Darrel Hadley

Grandview Elementary School
Old Central Building
1943 Hazel Fletcher Young
1945 Bertha Durnell
1946 Hazel Young
1948 Jena V. Holland

Present Building
1949 LaVar Kump
1951 Boyd McAffee
1954 Lewis Rawlinson
1959 Lincoln Card
1964 Dan Bird
1972 Vermont Harward
1973 Dan Bird

Joaquin Elementary
1939 Fred Strate
1954 H. D. Whatcott
1954 Floyd Breinholt
1956 Glen R. Brown
1967 Ned A. Allred
1972 John W. Bowen

Maeser School
1898 J. M. Jensen
1901 A. C. Sorenson
1902 Enoch Jorgensen
1908 Peter C. Peterson
1911 C. P. Olsen
1913 Reid Beck
1917 J. F. Wakefield
1919 E. V. Montague
1920 DeVere Childs
1921 Oscar Bjerregaard
1946 Marion J. Olsen
1954 Clinton Kanahele
1955 Marion J. Olsen
1958 Lincoln J. Card
1959 Ronald Last
1960 Marion J. Olsen
1961 James G. Bergera
1965 Monroe G. Gallier

Provost School
1949 Boyd McAffee
1951 Ross B. Denham
1953 Glen Brown
1956 Naomi Rowan
1958 Edith Stimpson

1965 Jim Bergera
1966 Grady Edenfield
1969 Edith Stimpson
1972 Ned Allred

Rock Canyon Elementary School
1964 Lincoln Card

Sunset View Elementary School
1959 Lewis Rawlinson

Timpanogos Elementary School
1892 S. P. Eggertson
1893 Ray E. Chase
1894 W. W. Billings
1895 John Foote
1896 A. C. Sorensen
1901 George Powelson
1915 F. M. Young
1920 B. H. Hyde
1924 Martin Whitbeck
1926 J. C. Moffitt
1928 Fred Markham
1929 Harvey Staheli
1948 Boyd McAffee
1949 Harvey Staheli
1966 Marvin Gunther

Wasatch Elementary School
1949 George Miller
1955 Ross B. Denham
1965 Vern Brimley
1967 William Geertsen

Principals of Provo Secondary Schools

Provo High School
1912 L. E. Eggertson
1915 Archie Thurman
1920 H. R. Atkins
1923 L. B. Harmon
1930 J. C. Moffitt
1937 Kenneth E. Weight, Sr.
1947 Delbert Tregeagle
1969 Ronald Last

Dixon Junior High School
1931 John F. Mower
1963 Ronald Last
1967 John Matthews
1969 Ray Warner
1970 John Matthews
1973 Neldon Mathews

Farrer Junior High School
1931 Jay W. Thornton
1953 Sherman W. Wing
1957 Gardner Snow
1967 Kenneth E. Weight, Jr.
1969 Lee Crab
1970 Kenneth E. Weight, Jr.

Central Junior High School
1956 Floyd Breinholt
1961 Ronald Last
(school discontinued)

Brigham Young University
1887 Karl G. Maeser
1892 Benjamin Cluff, Jr.
1903 George H. Brimhall
1921 Dr. Franklin S. Harris
1945 Dr. Howard S. McDonald
1951 Dr. Ernest L. Wilkinson
1971 Dr. Dallin H. Oaks

Utah Technical College
1941 H. E. Johnson
1945 Lorenzo Peterson
1946 Wilson Sorenson